Each Character A Picture the Chinese Written Language

by Wong Chon
Cheng Chung Hing

Peace Book • Hai Feng Publishing Co.

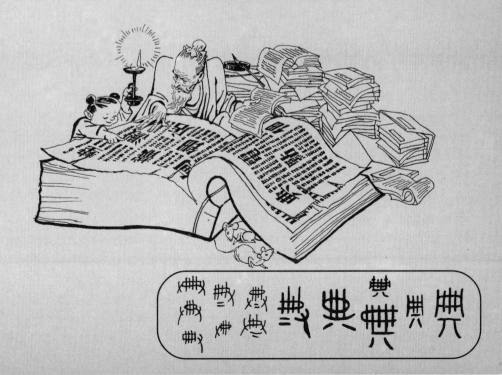

© Hai Feng Publishing Co., 1998
ISBN 962-238-250-9
HF-271-P

Each Character A Picture the Chinese Written Language

Compiled by	Wong Chon Cheng Chung Hing
Examined by	Cathryn Hope Clayton
Illustrated by	Cao Wei Ye
Edited by	Irene Li
Art Designed by	Ki-Coo Seto

Published by   Hai Feng Publishing Co.
                    Rm. 1502, Wing On House,
                    71 Des Voeux Road, Central
                    Hong Kong

Printed by   Maison D'editions Quaille
                    Room 15, 8/F, Block A, Wah Tat Industrial Center
                    8-10 Wah Sing Street
                    Kwai Chung
                    Hong Kong

Format   190 x 206 mm
Edition   First Edition July 1998
                    Second Edition July 2000

Preface

The American poet Ezra Pound once said, "The easiest language in the world for writing poetry is Chinese." And in the words of C. C. Cummings, another American poet, "Chinese poets are painters." This book, *Each Character A Picture the Chinese Written Language*, is one which uses words to explain and pictures to illustrate the form and structure of Chinese characters. Therefore, it is both a collection of poetry and a picture album, so to speak.

In China, words and pictures have always been bound together. From very early times, people talked about writing and painting having the same origin. If you examine the Chinese character 書 (shū) and 畫 (huà) (in the complex version), you will find that they share the same upper radical (component part) which resembles a writing brush in the grip of a hand. Thus, 書 and 畫 both convey the idea of working with a brush. In this sense, they are verbs. On the other hand, they also represent the products of working with a brush, and in that sense, they are nouns.

一 個 漢 字 一 幅 畫

It is not difficult to prove the relationship between the Chinese written character and poetry and painting. My friend, an overseas Chinese entrepreneur in Indonesia, Mr. Luo Haoran, or Ahmed Suriawinata, gave this example in his collection of prose *Watching the Clouds Gather*: "Consider the character 閒 which is quite interesting. It is a crescent moon seen through a crack between the two wings of a door." This may be a front door, a back door, or a window which opens in the middle. You push it open, raise your head and lift your eyes, and there in the sky is a clear, bright moon. You step out of the hall and immediately a pleasant, relaxed feeling fills your heart. To Mr. Luo, philology is a pastime only to be tended to after a day of battling in the business world, and yet his understanding of the Chinese character often surpasses that of a philologist. To him, the character 閒 not only presents a picture of the moon seen through the crack between the two panels of the door. It gives expression to an optimist's philosophy of life. I don't necessarily busy myself with what others are busy with; likewise, I may not feel at ease with something whereas others do. Only, when in the depth and quietude of night, one feels a peace and harmony within and without, only then can one be called a 閒人 , "a man at ease." Mr. Luo's explanation is well-founded. Xu Kai of the Song Dynasty, in his *Shuo Wen Xi Zhuan*, an explanatory book on *Shuo Wen Jie Zi*, China's earliest study of Chinese written characters and their forms and origins, had this to say in reference to the character 閒 : "The door is shut at night, yet one can still see the moon, for there's a slit in the door between the two wings."

Each Chinese character has a form of its own, representing a particular sound and a particular meaning, one at least. In other words, each character is a unity of form, sound and meaning. For every character, there is a form. There are as many "individuals" as there are characters. The student of Chinese must call on every one of the individuals if he or she is to really know the personality of each.

Learning Chinese is quite different from learning any other language. The

way of learning is different. In learning a Western language, for instance, you swallow a whole series of sounds, lock, stock and barrel. If you were to take a word apart, separating it into so many phonetic syllables, it would lose its meaning altogether. In learning Chinese, however, what you have to do is exactly that, not into so many syllables, but into so many characters. You learn first the characters, then the word. Take, for instance, the Chinese word 大學 (dà xué) which means "university". You first learn the words 大 and 學 separately since 大學 is formed by combining the two characters (you might call them elements of language). In meaning, 大學 has to do with both 大 and 學, and yet 大學 is not a simple case of 大 plus 學. It does not mean a big school (大的學校), nor a school for adults (大人的學校), and certainly not what was called (大家來學), everyone a student, a slogan in vogue during the decade of the so-called "Cultural Revolution". 大學 is the Chinese equivalent of the English word "university". But if you were to take the English word "university" and try to figure out its meaning based on the meanings of the five syllabic components u/ni/ver/si/ty, you would definitely get nowhere, because separately, these components have no meaning at all and certainly have nothing to do with what the word "university" means. So, the character forms the basis in learning Chinese, whereas the word or sentence forms the basis for learning a Western language. It is no wonder then that there should have been so many textbooks written since ancient times on learning Chinese characters, e.g. *Qian Zi Wen* (Learn A Thousand Characters) and *Bai Jia Xin* (One Hundred Family Names).

In Chinese, the character is the unit carrier of meaning whereas in English, it is the word that serves the same purpose. Each language in the world has its unique features, the same is true with the written script. One is always, consciously or unconsciously, interpreting another language and its written script on the basis of the characteristics of the language he or she first came into contact with in life. With respect to the Chinese language, one needs to study and appreciate its characters one by one, picture by picture, as one would in analysing and appreciating a work of art.

一 個 漢 字 一 幅 畫

The pictures as represented in the Chinese characters vary in complexity. Take the characters contained in this book. Some are as simple as 人 , 口 , 牛 , 羊 ; others as complicated as 雙 , 養 , 喜 , 聲 . Whether simple or complicated, they are each a picture and a poem. Of course, one cannot expect everyone to agree in their analyses of each and every character, just as people couldn't totally agree, in fact they might totally disagree, in their understanding and interpretation of a painting or a poem. Once a painting or a poem has been made public, the copyright, materially speaking, belongs to the work's creator; spiritually, however, it belongs to the whole society. Regardless of whether the poet or painter agrees or disagrees, the reader or viewer would have his own appreciation of the work on the basis of his or her own understanding. The same holds true, more or less, for the written script. It is your right to create the written character, it is my right to interpret it. Take the case of 章 (zhāng). Its original meaning was "the end", "conclusion", or "a temporary close of something." The book *Shuo Wen* says, "When the music finishes, it's a 章, which is made up of 音 (yīn, meaning music) and 十 (shí, meaning ten), for 十 is the limit of numbers." Chinese think of 十 as to mean "many", "complete"or "perfect." Hence the idiom 十全十美, meaning "perfect in every way", and the idiom of the drinkers wager 十滿大堂 , meaning "ten, the largest of all". When a melody reaches its end, one might say "the music has reached 十 (ten)". So, to say that the character 章 is the combination of 音 and 十 seems more like the original intent of the word's creator. And yet, 99% of the people consider 章 to be the combination of 立 and 早. In both the *Comprehensive Dictionary of Chinese Characters* and the *Comprehensive Dictionary of Chinese Words*, two authoritative dictionaries of the day, 章 is listed in the section under the radical 立 and not the section under the radical 音 or 十. Even people surnamed 章, when introducing themselves, choose to define their surname as 章 , 立 plus 早 .

There is yet another well-known example, the character 東 . This was originally written as 橐. Inscribed on oracle bones, it resembled a bag tied up at both ends. Later, an explanatory note in *Shuo Wen* put it as "the sun half way up the tree," indicating that the sun has newly risen over the horizon and has not

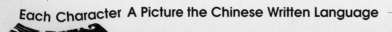

yet reached the top of the tree. When the sun reaches a height above the top of the tree, it is represented by the character 杲, and when it has sunk to below the bottom of the tree, it is represented by the character 杳. Thus, the three characters 橐, 杲, 杳 form a series illustrating the cycle from sunrise to sunset. *Shuo Wen's* explanation of the character 橐 therefore, seems quite acceptable. We might call the early explanations orthodox, and the later ones, common. Orthodox or common, they both serve to depict the origin of the Chinese character. We certainly shouldn't criticise those who describe 章 as a combination of 立 and 早, or the one who said that 橐 indicates "the sun is half way up the tree". Nevertheless, there has to be a limit to how common you can get. For instance, we must not imitate the fortune teller who does his job by taking apart and analysing the component parts of a character. That is not science. In this respect, this book *Each Character A Picture the Chinese Written Language* has achieved a good balance between the orthodox and the common. In present-day terms, this little book is both interesting and scientific.

For some time now, a theory has been going around among linguistic circles to the effect that all written languages in the world have to go through a process of elevation from being pictographic to ideographic to phonetic. According to this theory, the phonetic written language is the most developed of the three because it no longer has any link with meaning but only with sound. Thus, with only a small number of letters, one can spell out all the words there are. Judging by this standard, the Chinese character which remains at the ideographic stage is naturally not up to the standard of a developed language. A great man therefore pointed out that "The Chinese character must be reformed. It must follow the common orientation of the world's languages, that is the use of phonetic alphabet to replace the characters." However, it seems that the pictographic feature of the Chinese character cannot be changed overnight. Moreover, in this era, as the computer step by step enters every organization, every office room, every school and even every home, the unique pictographic feature of the Chinese character is more and more demonstrating its superiority. Thousands upon thousands of Chinese character-pictures have made their way to the computer terminal at a speed which equals, if not surpasses, that of the phonetic languages. They not only record the history of the Chinese civilization but serves the present-day purpose of uniting the Chinese nation and maintaining the country's unification. The Chinese written character and the Chinese nation share a common fate. If you wish to learn about this nation and its history and culture, you would find it hard to fulfil that wish without learning the characters.

Each Character A Picture the Chinese Written Language is written for those non-Chinese who intend to explore the secrets of the Chinese civilization. It is somewhat like a guidebook, listing more than a hundred cultural sites. Like the looking glass in *Alice in Wonderland*, the characters depicted in this book will take the tourist into the kaleidoscopic world that is Chinese culture. For people who are just beginning to have any contact with China, imagine yourself still inside a room, but with the help of this book, you will see "through the crack in the door" the clear, bright moon outside, or even the stars twinkling in the sky.

by Cheng Xianghui
Dean of College of Chinese Language
University of Macao
June 4, 1998

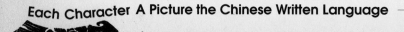

Contents

Each Character A Picture the Chinese Written Language

ān

(peaceful; quiet; calm)

This character is comprised of two parts: the outer portion is a house (⌂). Inside the house there is a seated, or kneeling woman (女) facing towards the left. Imagine, when the door to the house is shut, how peaceful and comfortable it is within! "A woman stays inside the house" has long been considered the condition of peace, the earliest known meaning of this particular pictograph.

安定	āndìng	stable; settled
安分	ānfèn	be low abiding
安好	ānhǎo	safe and sound; well
安靜	ānjìng	quiet; peaceful
安全	ānquán	safe; secure
安慰	ānwèi	comfort

安分守己
ān fèn shóu jǐ
keep one's duty and be self-restrained
i.e., act properly according to one's status

安居樂業
ān jū lè yè
live and work in peace and contentment

安然無恙
ān rán wú yāng
safe and sound
i.e., (escape) unscathed

安如泰山
ān rú Tài Shān
as secure as Mount Taishan

安不忘危
ān bú wàng wēi
mindful of possible danger in time of peace

Example:

祝你一路平安！
Zhù nǐ yí lù píngān!
Have a good trip!

bā
(eight)

八

The character 八 seems very simple. Yet, it is a combined representation which shows one thing being divided or parted into two halves. So originally 八 meant "divide" or "part". But later the meaning of "divide" was completely lost. 八 came to mean the number "eight" only because of its sound, which has nothing to do with the original meaning. 八 is also a radical. Most Chinese characters formed with 八 have something to do with the meaning of "divide".

八成	bāchéng	eighty percent
八方	bāfāng	the eight points of the compass; all directions
八仙	bāxiān	the "Eight Immortals" (in the legend)
八度	bādù	octave
八卦	bāguà	the Eight Diagrams (eight combinations of three whole or broken lines formerly used in divination
八月	bāyuè	August

八方呼應
bā fāng hū yìng
respond from all sides

八方支援
bā fāng zhī yuán
help from all quarters

八面玲瓏
bā miàn líng lóng
manage to please everybody

八十歲學吹打
bā shí suì xué chuī dǎ
learn to pipe and drum at the age of eighty

i.e., never too old to learn

八仙過海，各顯神通
bā xiān guò hǎi, gè xiǎn shén tōng
like the Eight Immortals crossing the sea, each one showing his or her special prowess

Example:

我買了八本中文書。
Wǒ mǎile bā běn zhōngwén shū.
I bought eight Chinese books.

bái

(white)

白

The original meaning of 白 is brightness. In the oracle bones, it is a picture of a fire burning with a bright ring surrounding it. Later it evolved to mean clarity, clearness.

白菜	báicài	Chinese cabbage
白癡	báichī	idiocy
白飯	báifàn	plain cooked rice
白費	báifèi	waste
白宮	báigōng	the White House
白色	báisè	white (colour)
白天	báitiān	daytime ; day
白銀	báiyín	silver

Each Character A Picture the Chinese Written Language

白璧無瑕
bái bì wú xiá
flawless white jade
i.e., impeccable moral integrity

白費心思
bái fèi xīn sī
to rack one's brains in vain

白駒過隙
bái jū guò xī
like glimpsing white colt flashing past a chink in the wall
i.e., time flies

白日做夢
bái rì zuò mèng
daydream

白頭偕老
bái tóu xié lǎo
remain a devoted couple to the end of their lives

白日不做虧心事，夜半敲門心不驚
bái rì bú zuò kuī xīn shì, yè bàn qiāo mén xīn bù jīng
A clear conscience laughs at false accusations.

Example:

她聽到這個消息頓時臉色蒼白。
Tā tīng dào zhèi ge xiāoxi dùnshí liǎnsè cāngbái.
She went as white as sheet when she heard the news.

běn
(the root of a plant ;
foundation)

本

When an additional short stroke being put near the base of the character (木)
"木 mù: originally meant tree", it is to emphasize where the roots of the tree is.
So, "root" is the original meaning of 本. It extends to the foundation for all the
things. From the meaning of "foundation", it also extends for meaning of "one's
own".

本能	běnnéng	instinct
本土	béntǔ	one's native country
本意	běnyì	original meaning
本國	běnguó	one's own country
本錢	běnqián	capital
本人	běnrén	me; myself ; oneself
本性	běnxìng	natural instincts
本源	běnyuán	origin; source

Each Character A Picture the Chinese Written Language

本固枝榮
běn gù zhī róng
When the root is firm, the branches flourish.

本末倒置
běn mò dào zhì
take the branch for the root

i.e., put the cart before the horse

本地薑不辣
běn dì jiāng bú là
Local ginger is not peppery.

i.e., Familiarity diminishes appreciation.

本來面目
běn lái miàn mù
true colour

i.e., true features

本鄉本土
běn xiāng běn tǔ
one's native land

i.e., one's hometown

Example:

助人是快樂之本。
Zhù rén shì kuàile zhī běn.
Helping people is the foundation of happiness.

bǐ

(compare; close to)

比

This character originally shows two people standing together facing towards the right ($\textit{ff}$) , very close to each other, giving us the original meaning of "close". Over time it has evolved and acquired the additional meanings of "compare"— as in "compare and contrast"— as well as "metaphor".

Clearly, though "close" is the original meaning of 比 , as we can see from the well-known verse from "*Du Shaofu Zhi Ren Shuzhou*" by Wángbó : " 海內存知己，天涯若比鄰 " (Keeping good friends in mind wherever they roam, even to the ends of the earth, you would feel them as close as next door.)

比較	bǐjiào	compare; contrast
比率	bǐlǜ	rate; ratio
比鄰	bǐlín	next-door neighbour
比如	bǐrú	for example; for instance; such as
比賽	bǐsài	competition; match
比喻	bǐyù	metaphor

比比皆是
bí bǐ jié shì
one can be found everywhere

比肩而事
bǐ jiān ér shì
work shoulder to shoulder

比翼雙飛
bǐ yì shuāng fēi
fly side by side

比上不足，比下有餘
bǐ shàng bù zú, bǐ xià yǒu yú
One man may fall short of the best but be better than the worst.

無可比擬
wú kě bǐ nì
beyond compare
i.e., incomparable; matchless

Example:

來，我倆比一比！
Lái, wóliǎ bǐ yì bǐ!
Come on, let's have a competition!

bǐ
(pen)

筆

This was originally an ideogram. In the oracle bones, the upper right part of the character is a hand (⽁), and the left side forms the shape of a pen (⼂) represents the body of the pen, and the triangular shape at the bottom represents the head of the pen. The character underwent numerous changes. In regular script it has lost most of its resemblance to a pen, but interestingly, in simplified Chinese, 筆 is written as 笔, a combination of 竹 "bamboo" and 毛 "hair" which is exactly what a Chinese pen is made of.

筆法	bǐfǎ	technique of writing
筆跡	bǐjì	a person's handwriting
筆譯	bǐyì	written translation
筆錄	bǐlù	take down (in writing); record
筆名	bǐmíng	pen name
筆墨	bǐmò	pen and ink; words
筆試	bǐshì	written examination
筆戰	bǐzhàn	written polemics

筆底生花
bí dǐ shēng huā
Flowers spring up under one's pen.

i.e., have great literary talent

筆飛墨舞
bǐ fēi mò wǔ
The pen flies, the ink dances.

i.e., write quickly

筆耕度日
bǐ gēng dù rì
making a living by writing

筆劍唇槍
bǐ jiàn chún qiāng
The pen is as sharp as the sword and the tongue as the spear.

筆墨官司
bǐ mò guān si
written polemics

筆墨難罄
bǐ mò nán qìng
hard to describe by pen and ink

i.e., beyond description

Example:

這枝筆是一位中國朋友送我的禮物。
Zhè zhī bǐ shì yí wèi Zhōngguó péngyǒu sòng wǒ de lǐwù.
This pen is a gift from a Chinese friend.

bīng
(ice)

冰

In the oracle bones this character is in the form of two persons (⌃) like protruding ice pieces, so originally 冰 was a pictographic character. But later a 水 "water" radical was added to it (𣲺), showing that "ice" is made of "water".

冰雹	bīngbáo	hail
冰川	bīngchuān	glacier
冰袋	bīngdài	ice bag
冰島	bīngdǎo	Iceland
冰冷	bīnglěng	ice-cold
冰山	bīngshān	iceberg

冰天雪地
bīng tiān xuě dì
a world of ice and snow

冰消瓦解
bīng xiāo wǎ jiě
to melt like ice and break like tiles

冰炭不相容
bīng tàn bù xiāng róng
as incompatible as ice and hot coals

冰凍三尺，非一日之寒
bīng dòng sān chǐ, fēi yí rì zhī hán
It takes more than one cold day for the river to freeze three feet deep.

i.e., The trouble has been brewing for quite some time.

Example:

這水冰手。
Zhè shuǐ bīng shǒu.
This water is freezing cold.

bù

步

(step; pace; walk)

步 is comprised of two feet. In the oracle bones, the upper part is a left foot with the big toe pointing upwards (𝖄) and the lower part is a right foot with the big toe also pointing upwards (𝖄) , but in the other direction. Two feet moving forwards one after another signifies "walking forward"; this is the original meaning of 步 "step". It is also used as a noun, and as an old unit of measurement. The modern version of 步 still keeps the "foot" in the upper part, but the lower part of it has been changed completely into another form.

步步	bùbù	step by step
步兵	bùbīng	infantry
步調	bùdiào	pace
步槍	bùqiāng	rifle
步行	bùxíng	walk; go on foot
步驟	bùzhòu	step; move
步子	bùzi	step; pace
散步	sànbù	take a walk

Each Character A Picture the Chinese Written Language

步步高升
bù bù gāo shēng
be promoted step by step

步調一致
bù diào yí zhì
march in step

i.e., act in unison

步人後塵
bù rén hòu chén
follow in somebody's footsteps

步武先賢
bù wǔ xiān xián
tread in the footsteps of the worthies of the past

步步為營
bù bù wéi yíng
advance gradually and entrench oneself at every step

Example:

只有幾步就到家了！
Zhíyǒu jǐ bù jiù dào jiā le.
We're only a few steps away from home now!

căo

(grass)

草

The upper part of 草 is a pictograph for grass (ΨΨ resembling two blades of grass) which is the origin of this character, and is also a radical for grass or plants. The lower part 早 was added as a phonetic later.

草地	căodì	grassland
草稿	cáogăo	rough draft
草緑	căolǜ	grass green
草帽	căomào	straw hat
草莓	căoméi	strawberry
草棚	căopéng	thatched shack
草皮	căopí	sod
草坪	căopíng	lawn
草率	căoshuài	careless
草圖	căotú	sketch
草藥	căoyào	medicinal herbs
草約	căoyuē	draft treaty
草原	căoyuán	prairie

草草過目
cáo cǎo guò mù
glance over
草草了事
cáo cǎo liǎo shì
get a job done any old way
草草收場
cáo cǎo shōu chǎng
hastily wind up a matter
草菅人命
cǎo jiān rén mìng
treat human life as if it were not worth a straw
草莽英雄
cáo mǎng yīng xióng
a hero from the bush
草木皆兵
cǎo mù jié bīng
see every bush and tree as an enemy
草動知風向
cǎo dòng zhī fēng xiàng
A straw shows which way the wind blows.

Example:

他在園子裡鋤草呢。
Tā zài yuán zi lǐ chú cǎo ne.
He is hoeing up weeds in the garden.

chū

(go out; come out)

The original character 出 is a combination of two parts: the lower part is a line which curves upwards indicating a doorway or a cave-dwelling (⋃) ; the upper part is a foot with the toe pointing upwards (∀) , implying the foot moving across threshold of the door or cave-dwelling. As the character developed, it took the form of two mountains overlapping. The original meaning of the character was "to go out" or "to come out"; later it extended to mean "exceed", "produce" etc.

出版	chūbǎn	come off the press; come out; publish
出兵	chūbīng	dispatch troops
出差	chūchāi	be on business
出產	chūchǎn	produce
出醜	chūchǒu	make a fool of oneself
出發	chūfā	set out
出境	chūjìng	leave the country
出口	chūkǒu	speak out; export; exit; utter

出爾反爾
chū ěr fán ěr
go back on one's word

出乎意料
chū hū yì liào
contrary to one's expectations

出口成章
chū kǒu chéng zhāng
Words flow from the mouth as from the pen of a master.

i.e., speech full of elegance

出類拔萃
chū lèi bá cuì
stand out from among one's fellows

出生入死
chū shēng rù sǐ
go through fire and water

i.e., risk one's life

出奇制勝
chū qí zhì shèng
achieve the victory through the unusual means

出污泥而不染
chū wū ní ér bù rǎn
come out of the mud unsoiled

i.e., emerge unstained from the filth

出其不意，攻其無備
chū qí bú yì, gōng qí wú bèi
do what one does not expect and strike when one is unprepared

Example:

今天早上他出城了。
Jīntiān zǎoshang tā chū chéng le.
He went out of the town this morning.

一個漢字一幅畫

chū
(beginning)

初

This is an ideogram formed by two pictograms: on the left side is 衣 "clothes" and on the right side is 刀 "knife". Combined these elements suggest using a knife to tailor new clothes, which in turn stands for the "beginning" of the process of making clothes. Gradually, it was generalized to mean "the beginning" of all things.

初步	chūbù	initial
初次	chūcì	the first time
初等	chūděng	elementary
初婚	chūhūn	first marriage
初交	chūjiāo	new acquaintance
初戀	chūliàn	first love
初期	chūqī	initial stage

初出茅廬
chū chū máo lú
just come out of one's thatched cottage
i.e., at the beginning of one's career; young and inexperienced

初露鋒芒
chū lù fēng máng
display one's talent for the first time

初生之犢不怕虎
chū shēng zhī dǔ bú pà hǔ
New born calves are not afraid of tigers.

i.e., Young people are fearless.

初入世途
chū rù shì tú
start in life

初衷不改
chū zhōng bù gǎi
New born calves are not afraid of tigers.

i.e., Young people are fearless.

Example:

初學漢語，要有耐心。
Chū xué Hànyǔ, yào yǒu nàixīn.
It requires much patience in learning Chinese at the beginning.

一個漢字一幅畫

cóng

(from)

From early oracle bones, we can see two people standing close together, facing towards the left (从) , one person following the other. So "follow" is the original meaning of this character. Then, by extension and evolution the meaning shifts towards "obedient" and "from" in the sense of "He is from another village"; also "accessory" in the sense of "following in the footsteps of another person", i.e., an "accessory to a crime".

從此	cóngcǐ	from now on
從屬	cóngshǔ	to be subordinate to
從前	~~cóngqián~~	~~before~~
從事	cóngshì	to be engaged in
從頭	cóngtóu	from the beginning

從古到今
cóng gǔ dào jīn
from ancient times to the present

從一而終
cóng yī ér zhōng
to be faithful to one's husband unto death

從善如流
cóng shàn rú liú
to follow good advice as naturally as the river follows its course

從長計議
zóng cháng jì yì
need further consideration

Example:

您從哪兒來？
Nín cóng nǎr lái?
Where are you from?

一個漢字一幅畫

diǎn

(law)

典

This character is comprised of (⊞) on the top half and two "hands" (⼡ ⼢) on the bottom half, signifying books/letters being held in a pair of hands. Later the form of the character was changed by replacing the hands with a (兀)—something like what we call a bookshelf nowadays. This shows that the 冊 (cè: books) on the bookshelf are also called 典 (diǎn). So the original meaning for "diǎn" was "important/model books", as nowadays we still say 經典 (jīng diǎn: classics) or 藥典 (yào diǎn : medical classics). From the meaning "classics", it has also been extended to mean "law" or "system".

典範	diǎnfàn	model; example
典故	diǎngù	allusion
典籍	diǎnjí	ancient codes and records
典禮	diánlǐ	ceremony
典型	diǎnxíng	typical case
典雅	diányǎ	refined; elegant

典型示範
diǎn xíng shì fàn
show typical examples from real life

典雅可傳
diǎn yǎ kě chuán
be refined and worthy of being perpetuated

典章制度
diǎn zhāng zhì dù
(old) laws and institutions

典型人物
diǎn xíng rén wù
a typical character

Example:

我買了一本漢英詞典。
Wǒ mǎi le yì běn Hàn-Yīng cí diǎn.
I bought a Chinese-English Dictionary.

dōng

(east)

According to the famous philologist 許慎 "Xu Shen", this character is comprised of 日 "the sun" and 木 "tree". The sun rises in the center of the tree, indicating the direction is due "east". But later experts pointed out that the character 東 in the oracle bones looks like a big bag with its both ends tied ( ), so the original meaning should be " 東西 " (東西 dōng xi: thing). As the character developed and people could no longer discern the original form of "bag", the character also came to mean "the east".

東北	dōngběi	northeast
東方	dōngfāng	the east
東風	dōngfēng	east wind
東漢	Dōng Hàn	the East Han Dynasty
東南亞	Dōngnán Yà	the Southeast Asia
東歐	Dōng Ōu	Eastern Europe
東西	dōngxi	thing

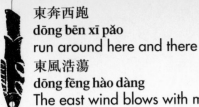

東奔西跑
dōng bēn xī pǎo
run around here and there

東風浩蕩
dōng fēng hào dàng
The east wind blows with mighty power.

東拉西扯
dōng lā xī chě
talk at random

東鄰西舍
dōng líng xī shè
next door neighbours

東風壓倒西風
dōng fēng yā dǎo xī fēng
The East Wind prevails over the West Wind.

Example:

他住在東部海岸地區。
Tā zhù zai dōngbù hǎi'àn dìqū.
He lives on the east coast.

dōng
(winter)

冬

Originally this character pictured a thread of silk which was knotted at both ends. It was used to indicate that a thing or an incident had come to an end, and it also implied the season at the end of the year. The sign (大)which means "ice", was added to (夅). Therefore (夅) which later developed into 冬, came to mean winter, the last season of the year. You can still find traces of the original meaning: when the silk radical "糸" is added to 冬, it becomes 終, which winter means "the end ".

冬天	dōngtiān	winter
冬季	dōngjì	winter (season)
冬菇	dōnggū	winter mushrooms
冬瓜	dōngguā	wax gourd
冬衣	dōngyī	winter clothes
冬至	dōngzhì	the Winter Solstice (the 22nd solar term)
冬装	dōngzhuāng	winter dress

Each Character A Picture the Chinese Written Language

冬暖夏涼
dōng nuǎn xià liáng
cool in summer and warm in winter

冬去春來
dōng qù chūn lái
Spring follows winter.

冬夏常青
dōng xià cháng qīng
to remain green throughout the year

冬春之交
dōng chūn zhī jiāo
at the end of winter and the beginning of spring

Example:

你的生日在冬天。
Nǐ de shēngrì zài dōngtiān.
Your birthday comes in the winter.

duō

(winter)

多

This is an ideogram. It is formed by two "夕", one on top of the other. It signifies that days and nights are changing forever. This meaning then implied the idea of 多 "a lot".

The original meaning of 多 was an antonym of 少 "a little". Later, another meaning was added, which is "more". In Chinese, "two hundred more" means "more than two hundred".

多邊	duōbiān	multilateral
多變	duōbiàn	changeable
多病	duōbìng	susceptible to diseases
多寡	duōguǎ	number
多虧	duōkuī	thanks to

多才多藝
duō cái duō yì
versatile

多愁善感
duō chóu shàn gǎn
sentimental

多如牛毛
duō rú niú máo
countless

多災多難
duō zāi duō nàn
be dogged by bad luck

多勞多得
duō láo duō dé
more pay for more work

多謀善斷
duō móu shàn duàn
resourceful and decisive
i.e., sagacious and resolute

Example:

多虧你的幫助。
Duō kuī nǐ de bāngzhù.
Thanks to your help.

ěr
(ear)

耳

The original character of 耳 "ear" just took the form of a person's ear, placing particular emphasis on the outer ear.

耳朵	ěrduo	ear
耳環	ěrhuán	earrings
耳光	ěrguāng	a slap on the face
耳機	ěrjī	earphone
耳鳴	ěrmíng	tinnitus
耳目	ěrmù	what one sees and hears
耳塞	ěrsāi	earplug
耳語	éryǔ	whisper
耳墜子	ěrzhuìzi	eardrop

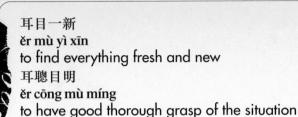

耳目一新
ěr mù yì xīn
to find everything fresh and new

耳聰目明
ěr cōng mù míng
to have good thorough grasp of the situation

耳濡目染
ěr rú mù rǎn
ears soaked and eyes dyed

i.e., be imperceptibly influenced by what one constantly sees and hears

耳熟能詳
ěr shú néng xiáng
What has been well-heard can be repeated in detail.

i.e., have heard many times

耳聞不如目見
ěr wén bù rú mù jiàn
Hearsay is not equal to observation.

Example:

不管我說什麼，他總是把我的話當耳邊風。
Bùguǎn wǒ shuō shénme, tā zǒng shì bǎ wǒdehuà dāngzuò ěrbiānfēng.
Anything I told he went in at one ear and out the other.

一個漢字一幅畫

fēn

(cut)

分

分 is comprised of two parts: the inside is a 刀 "knife" which means "to cut"; the outside is 八 which means something being separated. The idea of this character is to cut something with a knife —which signifies "to separate". From this, the meaning was extended to include " 分辨 "(fēnbiàn: to distinguish), as in " 真假難辨 " (zhēn jiǎ nán biàn: difficult to distinguish true or false) and the "branch" (of an organization, as in " 分店 " (fēndiàn: branch "of a shop").

分別	fēnbié	part; difference; separately
分佈	fēnbù	be distributed
分擔	fēndān	share responsibility
分割	fēngē	cut apart
分工	fēngōng	divide the work
分行	fēnháng	branch (of a bank)
分機	fēnjī	extension (telephone)
分居	fēnjū	(of a couple or members of a family) live apart

Each Character A Picture the Chinese Written Language

分崩離析
fēn bēng lí xī
fall apart (into pieces)

分辨是非
fēn biàn shì fēi
distinguish between right and wrong

分道揚鑣
fēn dào yáng biāo
each going his own way

分工合作
fēn gōng hé zuò
share out and cooperate with one another

分身不暇
fēn shēn bù xiá
unable to be in two places at the same time

分文不值
fēn wén bù zhí
not worth a cent

Example:

我們對這件事要一分為二來看。
Wǒmen duì zhèi jiàn shì yào yì fēn wéi èr lái kàn.
We should face this problem (matter) adopting a one-dividing-two attitude.

fū
(man; husband)

夫

夫 is also formed by adding a horizonal stroke above (个) "person", yet this horizonal stroke does not mean "head of the person". Rather, it means the hairpin in a man's hair. In ancient times, when a boy reached the age of 20, he had to bind his hair with a hairpin in a ritual initation, to be considered a grown up man. Therefore, the hairpin is the sign of "a grown up man", and this is also the original meaning of 夫 .

夫婦	fūfù	husband and wife
夫妻	fūqī	husband and wife
夫權	fūquán	authority of the husband
夫人	fūrén	lady; Madame; Mrs.
夫子	fūzǐ	an ancient form of address to a Confucian scholar or to a master by his disciples
丈夫	zhàngfū	husband
情夫	qíngfū	lover
懦夫	nuòfū	coward
農夫	nóngfū	farmer

Each Character A Picture the Chinese Written Language

夫唱婦隨
fū chàng fù suí
the husband singing, the wife accompanying
i.e., domestic harmony

夫婦之道
fū fù zhī dào
the proper relations between husband and wife

夫子自道
fū zi zì dào
The master speaks of himself.
i.e., One speaks of oneself.

夫妻無隔夜之仇
fū qī wú gé yè zhī chóu
There is no overnight hatred between man and wife.

Example:

你認為一夫一妻制怎麼樣？
Nǐ rènwéi yī fū yī qī zhì zěnmeyàng?
What do you think of the system of monogamy?

fù
(married woman)

From early inscriptions of this character found on oracle bones, we can see that on the left half of the pictograph there is something like a broom or duster (彐), while the right half derives from the character for woman (女). The idea thereby expressed is that a woman with a broom or duster in hand is a married woman. This character clearly shows that from the earliest of ancient times women were fixed within society in the role of being responsible for housework, just as men were expected to exert their strength in the fields, as shown by the character 男 (nán : man).

婦女	fùnǚ	woman
婦人	fùrén	married woman
婦幼	fùyòu	women and children
少婦	shàofù	young married woman
夫婦	fūfù	husband and wife

婦人之仁
fù rén zhī rén
a woman's kindheartedness

婦道人家
fù dào rén jiā
the fair sex

婦孺皆知
fù rǔ jié zhī
even women and children all know

婦人之見
fù rén zhī jiàn
views of a woman

i.e., short sighted or worthless views, not to be taken seriously

菁 粺 歸 婦

Example:

婦女能頂半邊天。
Fùnǚ néng dǐng bànbiān tiān.
Women can support half of heaven.

gān

(sweet ; pleasant)

甘

The pictograph for 甘 is a mouth with a line inside (⊟), representing food. Because the food has not been swallowed, but has been kept in the mouth, we know that it must taste good, or sweet. 甘 is also extended to mean "be perfectly happy to".

甘心	gānxīn	willingly
甘苦	gānkǔ	sweetness and bitterness
甘露	gānlù	sweet dew
甘休	gānxiū	be willingly to give up
甘泉	gānquán	fresh spring
甘願	gānyuàn	willingly; readily

甘拜下風
gān bài xià fēng
candidly admit defeat

甘瓜苦蒂
gān guā kǔ dì
The melon is sweet but the stalk is bitter.

甘棠遺愛
gān táng yí ài
Sweet memories left behind by a virtuous and capable official.

甘心情願
gān xīn qíng yuàn
be perfectly willing

甘言悅耳
gān yán yuè ěr
tickle sb's ear

Example:

他們同甘共苦，心心相印。
Tāmen tóng gān gòng kǔ, xīn xīn xiāng yìn.
They shared joys and sorrows, and were kindred spirits.

一 個 漢 字 一 幅 畫

gāo

(high)

高

高 is an adjective, which makes it very difficult to depict. Therefore ancient Chinese used "high fixtures" to represent the idea. In the oracle bones, (⿳) depicted a multi-story building, and thus represented the idea of "high".

高矮	gāo'ǎi	height
高潮	gāocháo	high tide
高大	gāodà	tall and big
高度	gāodù	altitude
高貴	gāoguì	noble
高級	gāojí	senior
高溫	gāowēn	high temperature

高高在上
gāo gāo zài shàng
stand high above masses

高官厚祿
gāo guān hòu lù
high position and handsome salary

高不可攀
gāo bù kě pān
too high to reach

高不成，低不就
gāo bù chéng, dī bú jiù
be unfit for a higher post but unwilling to take a lower one

高枕無憂
gāo zhěn wú yōu
shake up the pillow and have a good sleep

Example:

你的兒子長得很高。
Nǐ de érzi zhǎng dé hěn gāo.
Your son is very tall.

gōng

(work; labour)

工

工 is a pictograph. The form of the character on oracle bones seems like a carpenter's square or a ruler. The original meaning for this character is a carpenter's square.

工廠	gōngchǎng	factory
工程	gōngchéng	engineering; project
工地	gōngdì	building site
工夫	gōngfu	time; skill
工會	gōnghuì	labour union
工匠	gōngjiàng	craftsman
工人	gōngrén	worker
工作	gōngzuò	work; job
工商業	gōngshāngyè	industry and commerce

Each Character A Picture the Chinese Written Language

工力悉敵
gōng lì xī dí
be a match for each other in skill

工力深厚
gōng lì shēn hòu
remarkable craftsmanship

工詩善畫
gōng shī shàn huà
be well versed in painting and poetry

工欲善其事，必先利其器
gōng yù shàn qí shì, bì xiān lì qí qì
A workman must first sharpen his tools if he wishes to do his work well.

i.e., Good tools are prerequisite to a successful job.

Example:

工作之餘，我喜歡運動。
Gōngzuò zhī yú, wǒ xǐhuan yùndòng.
I like sports after work.

gǔ

(ancient; old)

古

A combination of 十 "ten" and 口 "mouth", which means there are many mouths. This implies words and wisdom being passed orally over generations and thus the meaning of "old" and "ancient" is derived.

古板	gúbǎn	old fashioned and inflexible
古代	gǔdài	ancient times; antiquity
古典	gúdiǎn	classical allusion; classical
古都	gǔdū	ancient capital
古怪	gǔguài	odd; strange
古迹	gǔjī	historical site
古籍	gǔjí	ancient books
古老	gúlǎo	ancient; age-old
古人	gǔrén	the ancients
古文	gǔwén	prose written in classical literary style

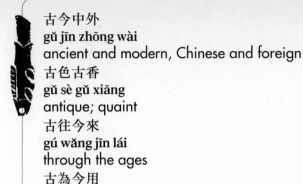

古今中外
gǔ jīn zhōng wài
ancient and modern, Chinese and foreign

古色古香
gǔ sè gǔ xiāng
antique; quaint

古往今來
gú wǎng jīn lái
through the ages

古為今用
gǔ wéi jīn yòng
make the past serve the present

古道熱腸
gǔ dào ré cháng
considerate and warmhearted
i.e., sympathetic

Example:

您喜歡這幅古畫嗎?
Nín xǐhuan zhè fù gǔ huà ma?
Do you like this ancient painting?

一 個 漢 字 一 幅 畫

guāng
(brightness;
light; glory)

光

We can see that the lower part of this character represents a person (〻) kneeling towards the right ; above this person is a fire illuminating the scene (业) . This clearly conveys the idea that it was fire that brought the light of awareness to mankind, which then lead the way to civilization.

光彩	guāngcǎi	lustre; splendour
光華	guānghuá	brilliance; splendour
光環	guānghuán	a ring of light
光潔	guāngjié	bright and clean
光臨	guānglín	presence (of a guest)
光明	guāngmíng	light
光榮	guāngróng	honour; glory

光明正大
guāng míng zhèng dà
open and aboveboard
i.e., just and honourable
光天化日
guāng tiān huà rì
in the light of the day
光陰似箭
guāng yīn sì jiàn
time flying like an arrow
光陰荏苒
guāng yīn rén rǎn
time passes very quickly
光宗耀祖
guāng zōng yào zǔ
making one's ancestors illustrious

Example:

兒童是世界的希望之光。
Értóng shì shìjiè de xīwàng zhī guāng.
Children are the light of our hope in this world.

hǎo

好

(good; fine; nice)

In the oracle bones, the left side of this character shows a kneeling woman holding a baby to her breasts (孖). This form of the character thus demonstrates that people in ancient times considered a woman with children to be superior to, and better than, a woman without children.

好吃	hǎochī	good to eat; delicious
好多	hǎoduō	a good many
好感	háogǎn	favourable impression
好看	hǎokàn	good looking
好人	hǎorén	good person
好玩兒	hǎowánr	amusing

Each Character A Picture the Chinese Written Language

好事多磨
hǎo shì duō mó
The road to happiness is strewn with setbacks.

好景不長
hǎo jǐng bù cháng
Good times don't last long.

好了瘡疤忘了疼
hǎo le cāngbā wàng le téng
When the wound is healed, one forgets the pain.

好自為之
hǎo zì wéi zhī
conduct oneself well

好事不出門，惡事傳千里
hǎo shì bù chū mén, è shì chuán qiān lǐ
Good deeds are never heard of outside door, but bad deeds are proclaimed for three hundred miles.

Example:

今天天氣真好。
Jīntiān tiānqì zhénhǎo.
The weather is really fine today.

一 個 漢 字 一 幅 畫

huǒ

(flame; fire)

火

火 is a pictographic character. As the oracle bones show, it pictures the shape of a flame rising into the air. 火 is a radical in other Chinese characters, (there are three forms of the "fire" radical: one is placed on the left side; the others are written on the bottom as a flattened 火, or as four dots); Chinese characters with this radical mostly have something to do with "fire" or "heat", or the functions of fire.

火把	huóbǎ	torch
火柴	huǒchái	match
火車	huǒchē	train
火光	huǒguāng	blaze
火海	huóhǎi	a sea of fire
火花	huǒhuā	spark
火雞	huǒjī	turkey
火箭	huǒjiàn	rocket
火山	huǒshān	volcano

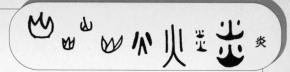

火上加油
huǒ shàng jiā yóu
add oil to the fire

火燒眉毛
huǒ shāo méi mao
fire burning the eyebrows

i.e., a matter of upmost urgency

火樹銀花
huǒ shù yín huā
a display of firewoods and a sea of lanterns

i.e., on a festival night

火中取粟
huǒ zhōng qǔ lì
pull sb's chestnuts out of the fire

i.e., be a cat's-paw

Example:

不能讓小孩子玩兒火！
Bùnéng ràng xiǎoháizi wánr huǒ!
Don't let children play with fire.

jí
(lucky; auspicious;
propitious)

吉

In the oracle bones, the upper part of this character is like a weapon (◊) and the lower part is like utensil (◻) used to store weapons. The combination of these two implies that when weapons are stored away, they are not being used, so there are fewer wars and less danger.

吉利	jílì	lucky
吉期	jíqī	wedding day
吉慶	jíqìng	auspicious; propitious
吉他	jítā	guitar
吉祥	jíxiáng	lucky
吉普車	jípǔchē	jeep

Each Character A Picture the Chinese Written Language

吉光片羽
jí guāng piàn yǔ
a fragment of a highly treasured relic
吉人天相
jí rén tiān xiàng
Heaven assists the good.
吉日良辰
jí rì liáng chén
an auspicious day
吉祥如意
jí xiáng rú yì
May you have good fortune according to your wishes.

Example:

七是我的吉祥數字。
Qī shì wǒ de jíxiáng shùzì.
Seven is my lucky number.

jiā

(family; home)

家

This is an associative character comprised of two parts: the upper portion relates to the meaning of "house" (⌂), while below the roof there is a pig (豕). In China, as in many other ancient societies, swine perhaps the earliest of all domesticated animals, along with dogs,were kept close to home. Therefore, a pig residing in or under a house became, through logical association, a symbol of the family's dwelling place, its "home", and by extension and permutation, the family home became the family itself.

家庭	jiātíng	the family home
家鄉	jiāxiāng	one's native place
家產	jiāchǎn	family property
家教	jiājiào	family education
家眷	jiājuàn	wife and children

家常便飯
jiā cháng biàn fàn
homely food

家家戶戶
jiā jiā hù hù
each and every family

家醜不可外揚
jiā chǒu bù kě wài yáng
Domestic scandals should not be made public.

家家有本難唸的經
jiā jiā yóu běn nán niàn de jīng
Every family has a skeleton in the cupboard.

Example:

她愛上了一個不回家的人！
Tā ài shang le yí gè bù huí jiā de rén!
She fell in love with one who doesn't go home!

jiàn

(see)

見

This character in the oracle bones represented a person kneeling on the ground facing right ( ). Above the head of the person was a big eye ( ) which gave the idea of someone watching someone else.

見報	jiànbào	to appear in the newspaper
見地	jiàndì	insight; judgment
見怪	jiànguài	mind; take offence
見解	jiànjiě	view; opinion
見聞	jiànwén	what one sees and hears
見識	jiànshi	experiences; knowledge
見外	jiànwài	regard sb. as an outsider
見效	jiànxiào	become effective
見笑	jiànxiào	laugh at (me or us)

Each Character A Picture the Chinese Written Language

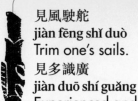

見風駛舵
jiàn fēng shǐ duò
Trim one's sails.

見多識廣
jiàn duō shí guǎng
Experienced and knowledgeable.

見仁見智
jiàn rén jiàn zhì
Different people, different views.

見微知著
jiàn wēi zhī zhù
from one small clue one can see what is coming

見異思遷
jiàn yì sī qiān
change one's mind the moment one sees something new

見義勇為
jiàn yì yǒng wéi
ready to take up arms for a just cause

Example:

我見過籃球明星米高佐敦。
Wǒ jiànguo lánqiú míngxīng Mǐgāozuǒdūn.
I have met the basket-ball star Michael Jordan.

一個漢字一幅畫

jiāo
(cross; associate
with; hand over)

交

This pictograph shows a man standing with his legs crossed (⽂) . The original meaning for it was "to cross the feet". Later, it was extended to mean "associate with", as "交朋友" (jiāo péng yǒu: make friends) or "hand over and take over" as "交貨" (jiāo huò: delivery) etc.

交叉	jiāochā	intersect; cross
交兵	jiāobīng	be at a war
交付	jiāofù	pay
交工	jiāogōng	hand over a completed project
交换	jiāohuàn	exchange
交集	jiāojí	(of different feelings) be mixed
交加	jiāojiā	(of two things) accompany each other
交界	jiāojiè	(of two or more places) have a common boundary
交融	jiāoróng	blend
交通	jiāotōng	traffic
交往	jiāowǎng	association
交易	jiāoyì	trade; deal

Each Character A Picture the Chinese Written Language

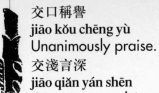

交口稱譽
jiāo kǒu chēng yù
Unanimously praise.

交淺言深
jiāo qiǎn yán shēn
Give sincere advice to people you hardly know.

交相輝映
jiāo xiāng huī yìng
add radiance and beauty to each other

交頭接耳
jiāo tóu jiē ěr
Speak in each other's ears.

水乳交融
shuí rǔ jiāo róng
blend as well as milk and water
i.e., be in perfect harmony

Example:

我來中國交了很多朋友。
Wǒ lái Zhōngguó jiāo le hěnduō péngyǒu.
I have made many friends since I came to China.

73

jiào

(teach; instruct)

教

The original character 教 showed a hand holding a stick on the right side (⃗), and on the lower left, a child with some kind of marks on its head from being beaten (⸙). This shows how education was in the old days, discipline was strict and, as shown in this character, often involved physical punishment.

教材	jiàocái	teaching material
教導	jiàodǎo	instruct
教皇	jiàohuáng	pope
教會	jiàohuì	church
教練	jiàoliàn	coach
教室	jiàoshì	class-room
教師	jiàoshī	teacher
教授	jiàoshòu	professor
教學	jiàoxué	education; teaching and studying
教訓	jiàoxun	lesson; moral
教育	jiàoyù	education

Each Character A Picture the Chinese Written Language

孺子可教
rú zǐ kě jiāo
The boy is worth teaching.

i.e., That's a good boy!

教導有方
jiào dǎo yǒu fāng
skillful in teaching and able to provide guidance

言傳身教
yán chuán shēn jiào
teach by precept and example

因材施教
yīn cái shī jiào
educate sb. according to his natural ability

教學相長
jiào xué xiāng zhǎng
Teaching benefits teacher and student alike.

i.e., Both teachers and students make progress by learning from each other.

Example:

他是一個兼職教師。
Tā shì yí ge jiānzhí jiàoshī.
He is a part-time teacher.

一 個 漢 字 一 幅 畫

jīn

(gold; bronze)

金

This character is a combination of an arrowhead and an ax; both of them are made of bronze and the two dots represent bronze ingots. The original form of the character is a combination of three parts: (♠) on the top of the character indicates "to cover"; under it is the earth (♣) indicates something hiding under the earth; and the two dots (⦂) by the side represent the mineral hiding under the earth. The original meaning of the character is metal.

金幣	jīnbì	golden coin
金剛鑽	jīngāng zuàn	diamond
金黃	jīnhuáng	golden yellow
金婚	jīnhūn	golden wedding
金庫	jīnkù	national treasury
金器	jīnqì	golden vessel
金錢	jīnqián	money
金融	jīnróng	finance; banking
金魚	jīnyú	golden fish

Each Character A Picture the Chinese Written Language

金科玉律
jīn kē yù lǜ
golden rule and precious

金碧輝煌
jīn bì huī huáng
looking splendid in green and gold

金迷紙醉
jīn mí zhǐ zuì
live an extravagant life

金銀財寶
jīn yín cái bǎo
gold, silver and other treasures

金屋藏嬌
jīn wū cáng jiāo
keep a mistress in a love nest

金玉良言
jīn yù liáng yán
invaluable advice

金玉其外，敗絮其中
jīn yù qí wài, bài xù qí zhōng
Rubbish coated in gold and jade.

金石為開
jīn shí wéi kāi
The utmost sincerity can soften even metal and stone.

i.e., Sincerity can make even metal or stone crack.

Example:

這家商店日進斗金。
Zhèi jiā shāngdiàn rì jìn dǒu jīn.
This shop is a regular gold-mine.

一 個 漢 字 一 幅 畫

kāi
(open)

開

The original character 開 is comprised of three parts: on the two sides was the double doors (門) ; in the middle of the doors there is a horizontal stroke representing the bolt (一) ; and under the bolt there is a pair of hands, indicating two hands removing the door bolt (廾) . The original meaning of 開 "kai" is "to open the door", but later came to be used also to mean "to open" in a general sense.

開車	kāichē	drive or start a car
開船	kāichuán	set sail
開動	kāidòng	start
開放	kāifàng	be open (to the public)
開花	kāihuā	blossom; bloom
開會	kāihuì	hold a meaning
開課	kāikè	school begins
開口	kāikǒu	open one's mouth; start to talk
開闊	kāikuò	open; wide

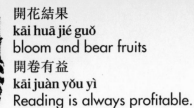

開花結果
kāi huā jié guǒ
bloom and bear fruits

開卷有益
kāi juàn yǒu yì
Reading is always profitable.

開誠相見
kāi chéng xiāng jiàn
treat somebody open-heartedly

i.e., meet or talk in all sincerity

開天闢地
kāi tiān pì dì
break fresh ground

開源節流
kāi yuán jié liú
to tap new resources of revenue and cut down expenditures

開張大吉
kāi zhāng dà jí
Let great prosperity attend the opening of a shop.

Example:

客人來了，快去開門！
Kèren lái le, kuài qù kāimén!
The guests have come, go to open the door quickly!

kàn
(look at;
watch; see)

看

This character is a combination of two parts: the upper part is a hand ( ), and the lower part is an eye ( ), meaning that man raises his hand above his eyes to look into the distance.

看病	kànbìng	(of a patient) to see a doctor
看出	kànchū	make out; see
看穿	kànchuān	see through
看待	kàndài	treat; regard
看到	kàndào	catch sight of; see
看法	kànfǎ	view
看望	kànwàng	call on; visit
看齊	kànqí	keep abreast with
看輕	kànqīng	underestimate
看得起	kàn de qǐ	think highly of

看家本領
kān jiā bén lǐng
one's special skill

看不順眼
kàn bú shùn yǎn
to one's dislike

看菜吃飯，量体裁衣
kàn cài chī fàn, líang tǐ cái yī
Fit one's appetite to the food served, and one's clothing to the figure.

i.e., adapt oneself to the circumstances

看人嘴臉
kàn rén zuí liǎn
live on another's favour

Example:

你看過 " 鐵達尼號 " 這部電影嗎 ?
Nǐ kànguo tiě dá ní hào zhè bù diànyǐng ma?
Have you seen the film *Titanic* ?

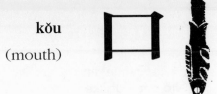

kǒu

(mouth)

This is a pictograph of a mouth with happy corners. The original meaning of 口 is "mouth", and from this meaning it is extended to represent "人口" (rén kǒu: "person's mouth"—"population"). "五口之家" (wú kǒu zhī jiā) "family of five mouths" means "a family with five persons". In addition, 口 also means "opening".

口碑	kǒubēi	public praise
口才	kǒucái	eloquence
口服	kǒufú	profess to be convinced
口袋	kǒudài	pocket
口號	kǒuhào	slogan
口渴	kóukě	thirsty
口試	kǒushì	oral examination
口味	kǒuwèi	personal taste

口口相傳
kóu kǒu xiāng chuán
go from mouth to mouth

口口聲聲
kóu kǒu shēng shēng
say again and again

口蜜腹劍
kǒu mì fù jiàn
honey on the lips and murder in the heart

口是心非
kǒu shì xīn fēi
affirm with one's lips but deny in one's heart

口誅筆伐
kǒu zhū bǐ fá
condemn both in speech and in writing

口服心不服
kǒu fú xīn bù fú
agree in words but not in mind

Example:

請你不要口是心非!
Qíng nǐ búyào kǒu shì xīn fēi!
Please don't say yes and mean no!

láo
(prison;
firm; durable)

牢

Looking at the original form of this character we can see it looks like an "ox" enclosed in a corral (⌷). As the character evolved, a mark was added which represented a big log leaning against the corral gate, so that ox would not be able to run out. In this way, the corral has became more sturdy. So the original meaning for 牢 was "corral for oxen". But the meaning came to encompass also "a place for caging a criminal", like 囚牢 (qiūláo) 檻牢 (jiānláo), "prison" or "jail". Since a "prison" or "jail" must be "firm", so 牢 can be used as an adjective as well as a noun .

牢固	láogù	firm; secure
牢記	láojì	keep firmly in mind
牢靠	láokào	strong; sturdy
牢牢	láoláo	firmly
牢籠	láolóng	cage; bonds
牢穩	láowěn	safe; stable
牢獄	láoyù	prison; jail

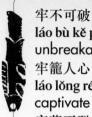

牢不可破
láo bù kě pò
unbreakable

牢籠人心
láo lǒng rén xīn
captivate the mind of men

牢落不群
láo luò bù qún
keeping oneself aloof

牢愁莫遣
láo chóu mò qiǎn
worried not knowing how to drive away melancholy

Example:

把繩子拴牢。
Bǎ shéngzi shuān láo.
Tie the rope fast.

lǎo

(old)

老

The oracle bones picture the character (老) as an old man facing the left, with a hunched back, long hair and a staff in his hand. Other characters relating to "old" or "elders" which are derived from this character includes 孝 (xiào: filial piety) and 長 (zhǎng: older).

老板	láobǎn	boss
老伴兒	lǎobànr	(of an old married) husband and wife
老本	láoběn	principal; capital
老成	lǎochéng	experienced; steady
老粗	lǎocū	uneducated person
老家	lǎojiā	native place
老練	lǎoliàn	seasoned; experienced
老年	lǎonián	old age
老實	lǎoshí	honest; frank
老師	lǎoshī	teacher
老鄉	lǎoxiāng	fellow-townsman
老腦筋	láonǎojīn	old-fashioned (or outmoded) way of thinking

86

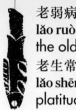

老弱病殘
lǎo ruò bìng cán
the old, weak, sick and disabled

老生常談
lǎo shēng cháng tán
platitudes; shopworn phrases

老當益壯
lǎo dāng yì zhuàng
old but vigorous

老馬識途
láo mǎ shí tú
The old horse knows the way.

老吾老以及人之老
lǎo wú lǎo yǐ jí rén zhī lǎo
Honour other aged people, as we honour our own.

老虎屁股摸不得
láo hǔ pì gu mò bù dé
like a tiger whose backside no one dares to touch

老王賣瓜，自賣自誇
lǎo wáng mài guā, zì mài zì kuā
Lao Wang the melon-seller praises his own goods.

i.e., to praise one's own work or wares

老驥伏櫪，志在千里
lǎo jì fú lì , zhì zài qiān lǐ
An old steed in the stable still aspires to gallop a thousand miles.

i.e., Old people may still cherish high aspirations.

Example:

他辦事老練。
Tā bànshì lǎoliàn.
He is experienced and works with a sure hand.

léi

(thunder)

雷

The ancient form of 雷 (⚡) depicts lightning accompanied by peals of thunder. Because a thunderclap sounds like drumming, it was depicted by four drum heads linked together. Later it was also topped with the radical 雨 ; the four drum heads were reduced to three, and gradually three were reduced to one, to produce the form we use today.

雷暴	léibào	thunderstorm
雷達	léidá	radar
雷電	léidiàn	thunder and lightning
雷動	léidòng	thunderous
雷聲	léishēng	thunderclap
雷陣雨	léizhènyǔ	thunder shower

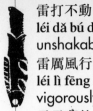

雷打不動
léi dǎ bú dòng
unshakable

雷厲風行
léi lì fēng xíng
vigorously and speedily

雷霆萬鈞
léi tíng wàn jūn
as powerful as a thunderbolt

雷聲大，雨點小
léi shēng dà, yú diǎn xiǎo
loud thunder but small raindrops
i.e., much said but little done

Example:

氣象預報今天會有雷雨。
Qìxiàng yùbào jīntiān huì yǒu léiyǔ.
The weather forecasts that there will be thunder and shower today.

lì
(power)

力

From the oracle bones we can see that the original form of (力) is like an ancient plough: the upper part, which curves at the bottom, is the wooden handle of a plough, and the lower part is its iron head. 力 is a pictograph of a plough and is used as the verb "to plough a field". Since ploughing the field requires strength, 力 then was used to express the meaning "force", "power" or "strength".

力量	lìliang	physical strength; power; force
力戒	lìjiè	strictly avoid
力氣	lìqi	physical strength; effort
力求	lìqiú	do one's best to
力圖	lìtú	try hard to; strive to
力爭	lìzhēng	work hard to
人力	rénlì	manpower; labour force

力薄才疏
lì bó cái sū
be deficient in strength and ability

力排眾議
lì pái zhòng yì
reject strongly different opinions

力不從心
lì bù cóng xīn
ability not equal to one's ambition

力所能及
lì suǒ néng jí
within one's power

力透紙背
lì tòu zhǐ bèi
(of poem etc.) profound in conception and succinct in language

力挽狂瀾
lì wǎn kuáng lán
make vigorous efforts to turn the tide

力爭上游
lì zhēng shàng yóu
strive for the best

Example:

這件事費了很大的力才做成。
Zhèi jiàn shì fèi le hěndà de lì cái zuò chéng.
This task requires a lot of effort to be done well.

mǎ

(horse) 馬

(🐎) is a pictographic character which depicts a horse with its head upwards, tail downwards and back to the right; it even depicts the hair. But as the character developed it lost these original pictographic features.

馬車	mǎchē	cart
馬鞭	mǎbiān	horsewhip
馬達	mǎdá	motor
馬隊	mǎduì	a team of horses
馬夫	mǎfū	groom
馬虎	mǎhu	careless
馬路	mǎlù	road; avenue
馬上	mǎshàng	at once
馬鈴薯	mǎlíngshǔ	potato
馬大哈	mǎdàhā	a careless person

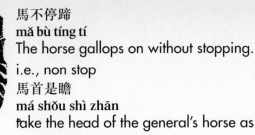

馬不停蹄
mǎ bù tíng tí
The horse gallops on without stopping.

i.e., non stop

馬首是瞻
má shǒu shì zhān
take the head of the general's horse as guide

i.e., follow sb.'s lead

馬仰人翻
má yǎng rén fān
men and horses thrown off their feet

i.e., to be turned upside-down

馬革裹屍
mǎ gé guǒ shī
be wrapped in a horse's hide after death

i.e., die on the battlefield

馬屁拍到馬腿上
mǎ pì pāi dào mǎ tuǐ shàng
flatter sb. the wrong way

Example:

你馬上就走嗎？
Nǐ mǎshàng jiù zǒu ma?
Are you leaving right away?

mǎi

(buy)

買

This is an associative compound character which originally combined the symbol for (网) "net", meaning "dredge", with a (贝)"shellfish", meaning "merchandise", indicating to "purchase" or "buy" the merchandise.

買辦	mǎibàn	comprador
買方	mǎifāng	the buying party
買價	mǎijià	buying price
買賣	mǎimài	buying and selling; commerce
買通	mǎitōng	to bribe; buy over
買主	máizhǔ	buyer

買空賣空
mǎi kōng mài kōng
speculate on the rise and fall of prices
買賣公平
mǎi mài gōng píng
to buy and sell at reasonable prices
買笑追歡
mǎi xiào zhuī huān
to buy laughter and seek pleasure
買櫝還珠
mǎi dú huán zhū
keep the glittering casket and give back the pearls to the seller
i.e., choose the wrong thing

Example:

我在香港買了很多東西。
Wǒ zài Xiānggǎng mǎi le hěnduō dōngxi.
I bought a lot of things in Hong Kong.

méi
(eyebrow)

This is a very good example of pictogram. The (ᑭᑭ) on top of eye (∅) represents the eyebrows.

眉筆	méibǐ	eyebrow pencil
眉毛	méimao	eyebrow; brow
眉目	méimù	features; looks; prospect of a solution
眉批	méipī	notes and commentary
眉梢	méishāo	the tip of the brow
眉頭	méitóu	brows
眉心	méixīn	between the eyebrows
眉宇	méiyǔ	forehead

眉開眼笑
méi kāi yǎn xiào
be all smiles
i.e., beam with joy

眉來眼去
méi lái yǎn qù
make eyes at each other

眉飛色舞
méi fēi sè wǔ
with dancing eyebrows and radiant face
i.e., enraptured

眉清目秀
méi qīng mù xiù
have delicate features

Example:

他聽到這個消息，高興得眉飛色舞。
Tā tīng dào zhèi ge xiāoxi, gāoxìng de méi fēi sè wǔ.
When he heard this news, he was delighted with dancing eyebrows and radiant face.

mén

(door; gate)

門

門 is a pictograph showing a set of double doors (𢩦). 門 is also a radical; the characters with this radical usually have something to do with the meaning of "door" or "gate".

門第	méndì	family status
門戶	ménhù	door; faction
門警	ménjǐng	police guard at an entrance
門徑	ménjìng	access; key
門檻	ménkǎn	threshold
門口	ménkǒu	entrance; doorway
門框	ménkuàng	door-frame
門廊	ménláng	porch
門簾	ménlián	door curtain
門面	ménmiàn	the facade of a shop
門牌	ménpái	(house) number plate
門徒	méntú	disciple; follower
門診	ménzhěn	outpatient service

門戶之見
mén hù zhī jiàn
sectarianism

門禁森嚴
mén jìn sēn yán
with the entrances heavily guarded

門庭若市
mén tíng ruò shì
The courtyard is like a market fair.

i.e., having many visitors

門當戶對
mén dāng hù duì
be well-matched in social and economic status (for marriage)

Example:

今天晚上七點我在大學門口等你。
Jīntiān wǎnshang qīdiǎn wǒ zài dàxué ménkǒu déng nǐ.
I'll wait for you at seven o'clock at the entrance of the university.

miàn

(face)

The original character of 面 shows the attempt to depict a man's face.

面對	miànduì	confront; face
面積	miànji	area
面頰	miànjiá	cheek
面具	miànjù	mask
面貌	miànmào	looks; features
面色	miànsè	complexion
面談	miàntán	speak to somebody face to face
面熟	miànshóu	look familiar
面子	miànzi	reputation

面不改色
miàn bù gǎi sè
not change colour
i.e., remain calm

面紅耳赤
miàn hóng ěr chì
be red in the face

面面俱到
miàn miàn jù dào
attend to each and every aspect of a matter

面和心不和
miàn hé xīn bù hé
remain friendly in appearance but estranged at heart

Example:

我們面對困難決不退縮。
Wǒmen miàn duì kùnnán juě bù tuìsuō.
We will never flinch from difficulties.

míng

(of a bird) to sing

鳴

鳴 is comprised of two pictographs: from the inscriptions on oracle bones, we can see clearly on the right side a bird stretching out its neck with its mouth open in song, and on the left side, a "mouth" radical which also suggests singing. So the original meaning for 鳴 is "bird sings". Later, from this meaning it was extended to include the sound made by any animal or insect, like 鹿鳴 "lù míng", 蟲鳴 "chóng míng": It has even come to be used to describe humans debating as in the saying "百家爭鳴"(bāi jiā zhēng míng : a hundred schools of thought contend.)

鳴鏑	míngdí	whistling
鳴笛	míngdí	whistle
鳴炮	míngpào	fire a shot
鳴槍	míngqiāng	fire a gun
鳴鼓	mínggǔ	beat a drum
鳴放	míngfàng	airing of views
雞鳴	jīmíng	the crow of a cock
耳鳴	ěrmíng	ringing in the ears

Each Character A Picture the Chinese Written Language

鳴鼓而攻
míng gǔ ér gōng
beat the drum and launch the attack
i.e., attack somebody publicly

鳴金收兵
míng jīn shōu bīng
beat the gong to call back the troops

i.e., call off the battle

鳴鑼開道
míng luó kāi dào
beat the gong to clear the way

i.e., clear the way for something

鳴冤叫屈
míng yuān jiào jū
complain and call for redress

i.e., voice one's discontent

不鳴則已，一鳴驚人
bù míng zé yǐ, yì míng jīng rén
not speak unless able to say something sensational

Example:

他這個人不鳴則已，一鳴驚人。
Tā zhèi ge rén bù míng zé yǐ, yì míng jīng rén.
He is a someone who does not speak unless able to say something sensational.

103

一個漢字一幅畫

mò
(tip; end)

末

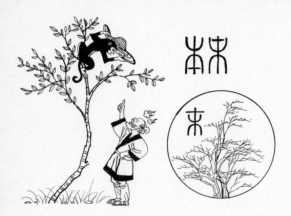

On the contrary of 本, 末 is constructed by adding a short stroke on the upper part of (朮) indicating the tip of the tree (朮). So the original meaning of 末 is "tip" or "end ", and it is also extended for the meaning of the things that is not important.

末代	mòdài	the last reign of a dynasty
末了	mòliǎo	in the end; last
末路	mòlù	dead end
末年	mònián	last years of a dynasty or reign
末期	mòqī	last phase
末日	mòrì	doomsday
末尾	mòwěi	end

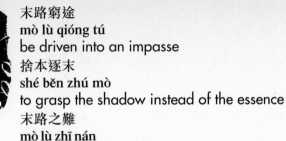

末路窮途
mò lù qióng tú
be driven into an impasse

捨本逐末
shé běn zhú mò
to grasp the shadow instead of the essence

末路之難
mò lù zhī nán
The arduousness of the last section of the journey.

i.e., The nearer to success, the more arduous.

本末倒置
běn mò dào zhì
take the branch for the root

i.e., put the cart before the horse

秋毫之末
qiū háo zhī mò
The tip of an animal's autumn hair.

Example:

今天是本學期的最末一天。
Jīntiān shì běn xuéqī de zuìmò yì tiān.
Today is the last day of this term.

mù

(tree; wood) 木

As we can see, this character is a pictograph of a tree ( ). The upper part is the treetop with its branches ( ), and the lower part is the roots ( ). The original meaning of this character is "tree", and it also stands for "wood" in general.

木材	mùcái	timber
木箱	mùxiāng	wooden box
木匠	mùjiang	carpenter
木屋	mùwū	log cabin
木星	mùxīng	Jupiter
木結構	mù jiégòu	timber structure

Each Character A Picture the Chinese Written Language

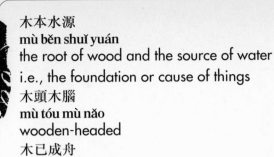

木本水源
mù běn shuǐ yuán
the root of wood and the source of water
i.e., the foundation or cause of things

木頭木腦
mù tóu mù nǎo
wooden-headed

木已成舟
mù yǐ chéng zhōu
The wood is already made into a boat.
i.e., What is done cannot be undone.

Example:

獨木不成林，人多力量大。
Dú mù bù chéng lín, rén duō lìliang dà.
A single tree does not make a forest, just as more people have more strength.

mù
(eye)

The drawing of () looks just like a real eye, and the original meaning of this character is precisely that. Later the curve indicating the iris of the eye was flattened, and the eye was turned to stand on its end before finally losing the shape of an eye.

目標	mùbiāo	objective; aim
目睹	mùdǔ	see with one's eyes
目光	mùguāng	sight
目的	mùdi	purpose
目擊	mùjī	see with one's own eyes
目錄	mùlù	catalogue
目前	mùqián	at present
目送	mùsòng	watch somebody go
目眩	mùxuán	dizzy

目不交睫
mù bù jiāo jié
not sleep at all

目不暇接
mù bù xiá jiē
The eye cannot take it all in.

目不斜視
mù bù xié shì
not look sideways

目瞪口獃
mù dèng kǒu dāi
be stunned

i.e., speechless

目光如豆
mù guāng rú dòu
with a vision as large as a bean

i.e., extremely short-sighted

目空一切
mù kōng yí qiè
look down upon everything

目濡耳染
mù rú ér rǎn
eyes soaked and ears dyed

i.e., be imperceptibly influenced by what one constantly sees and hears

目中無人
mù zhōng wú rén
consider everyone beneath one's notice

Example:

他目中無人，很沒禮貌。
Tā mù zhōng wú rén, hěn méi lǐmào.
He is very unpolite and consider everyone beneath his notice.

nán

(man; male)

男

The original character of 男 is a combination of two parts: the left side is a field (田), and the right side is a plough-like tool (𠃌). As ploughing the field was men's work in ancient times, the original meaning of 男 is "the strength in the field" or "man".

男人	nánrén	man
男女	nánnǚ	man and woman
男性	nánxìng	male
男朋友	nánpéngyǒu	boy friend
男子漢	nánzǐhàn	man; hero

男耕女織
nán gēng nǚ zhī
divisions of labour

男男女女
nán nán nǚ nǚ
men and women

男女平等
nán nǚ píng děng
equality of men and women

男女授受不親
nán nǚ shòu shòu bù qīng
It is improper for men and women to touch each other's hand in passing objects.

Example:

男孩子不一定比女孩子頑皮。
Nán háizi bù yídìng bǐ nǚ háizi wánpí.
Boys are not surely more naughty than girls.

niǎo
(bird)

鳥

鳥 is a pictograph of a bird with a head, wings, claws, and a tail, which are easily identifiable; later, the eyes were also added.

鳥瞰	niǎokàn	get a bird's eye view
鳥籠	niǎolóng	birdcage
鳥類	niǎolèi	birds
鳥槍	niǎoqiāng	fowling piece; birding piece
鳥獸	niǎoshòu	birds and beasts
鳥嘴	niáozuǐ	beak; bill

鳥盡弓藏
niǎo jìn gōng cáng
cast aside the bow once the birds are gone
鳥語花香
niáo yǔ huā xiāng
birds sing and flowers give forth their fragrance
鳥之將死，其鳴也哀
niǎo zhī jiāng sǐ, qí míng yě āi
When a bird is dying its cry is pitiful.
鳥為食亡，人為財死
niǎo wèi shí wáng, rén wèi cái sǐ
Birds die in pursuit of food, and human beings die in pursuit of wealth.
鳥無翅不飛，蛇無頭不行
niǎo wú chì bù fēi, shé wú tóu bù xíng
A bird without wings cannot fly and a snake without head cannot crawl.

Example:

我們在飛機上鳥瞰香港。
Wǒmen zài fēijī shang niǎokàn Xiānggǎng.
From the plane we had a bird's eye view of Hong Kong.

一個漢字一幅畫

niú

(ox; cow; bull)

牛

The original form of this character is the front view of an ox's head (𐊛). The two side of it which curved upwards are the horns of the ox, and the two strokes below the horn stretching out are ears. Later the ears were straightened to be a horizontal stroke and the form of the character became what we see today.

牛車	niúchē	oxcart
牛犢	niúdú	calf
牛角尖	niújiǎojiān	the tip of a horn
牛勁	niújìn	great strength
牛欄	niúlán	cattle pen
牛毛	niúmáo	ox hair
牛奶	niúnǎi	milk
牛脾氣	niúpíqi	stubbornness
牛肉	niúròu	beef
牛仔褲	niúzǎikù	jeans

牛刀小試
niú dāo xiǎo shì
a master hand's first small display
牛刀割雞
niú dāo gē jī
kill a chicken with a butcher's big knife
i.e., great talent used in petty things
牛馬不如
niú mǎ bù rú
worked even harder than oxen and horses
牛不喝水強按頭
niú bù hē shuǐ qiáng àn tóu
force an ox to bend its head to drink
i.e., force someone to do something
牛頭不對馬嘴
niú tóu bú duì má zuǐ
horses' jaws don't match cows' heads
i.e., incongruous

Example:

我習慣每天早上喝一杯牛奶。
Wǒ xíguàn měitiān zǎoshang hē yì bēi niúnǎi.
I get use to take a cup of milk every morning.

nǚ 女

(woman; girl)

In ancient times the position of women was as low as that of slaves, so the earliest known pictographs for woman show her in a bowing position with her arms crossed in front of her body (克). Subsequent developments show her in a kneeling position.

女皇	nǚhuáng	empress
女士	nǚshì	lady
女主人	nǚzhǔrén	hostess
女神	nǚshén	goddess
女巫	nǚwū	witch; sorceress
女郎	nǚláng	young woman; maiden
淑女	shūnǚ	gentlewoman

女中丈夫
nǚ zhōng zhàng fu
as a man amongst the woman folks
女大當嫁
nǚ dà dāng jià
A grown-up girl should marry at time.
女大十八變
nǚ dà shí bā biàn
A girl changes fast in physical appearance from childhood to adulthood.
女子無才便是德
nǚzǐ wú cái biàn shì dé
An unaccomplished woman is a virtuous woman.

Example:

她是一個獨身女子。
Tā shì yíge dúshēn nǚzǐ.
She is a single woman.

qì
(air; gas)

氣

The original pictograph was of clouds floating in the air. Three horizontal lines show the layers of the clouds with the middle layer shorter than the other two, implying emptiness (三). To avoid confusion with an other character 三 "three", people later gave the top and bottom layers a curly tail (气).

氣窗	qìchuāng	transom window
氣度	qìdù	tolerance; bearing
氣短	qìduǎn	be short of breath
氣氛	qìfen	atmosphere
氣憤	qìfèn	indignant
氣慨	qìkài	lofty quality; spirit
氣功	qìgōng	a system of deep breathing exercises
氣候	qìhou	climate
氣節	qìjié	integrity; moral courage
氣力	qìlì	effort; energy
氣流	qìliú	air current
氣呼呼	qìhūhū	in a huff

Each Character A Picture the Chinese Written Language

氣急敗壞
qì jí bài huài
flustered and exasperated
氣勢磅礴
qì shì páng bó
of great momentum
氣勢洶洶
qì shì xiōng xiōng
fierce
氣吞山河
qì tūn shān hé
imbued with a spirit that can conquer mountains and rivers
氣味相投
qì wèi xiāng tóu
have the same tastes and temperament

Example:

打開窗子透一透氣吧！
Dǎkāi chuāngzi tòu yí tòu qì ba!
Let's open the window to get some fresh air!

qǔ
(take; get)

取

取 is an associative compound character. On the left side it is an "ear" ( ) and on the right side a "hand" ( ). As in ancient times the war prisoners would have their left ears to be lopped off as testimony to their military exploits, so the original meaning of "take" is "to cut off the left ear"; from this the character was also extended to express the present meaning "take", "get" or "fetch".

取代	qǔdài	replace
取道	qǔdào	by way of
取得	qǔdé	gain; obtain
取締	qǔdí	outlaw
取經	qǔjīng	learn from sb. else's experience
取決	qǔjué	depend on
取暖	qúnuǎn	warm oneself
取勝	qǔshèng	win victory
取消	qǔxiāo	cancel
取笑	qǔxiào	make fun of

Each Character A Picture the Chinese Written Language

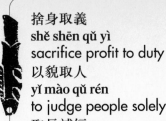

捨身取義
shě shēn qǔ yì
sacrifice profit to duty

以貌取人
yǐ mào qǔ rén
to judge people solely by their appearance

取長補短
qǔ cháng bǔ duǎn
learn from others' strong points to offset one's weakness

取之不盡，用之不竭
qǔ zhī bú jìn, yòng zhī bù jié
inexhaustible

取之於民，用之於民
qǔ zhī yú mín, yòng zhī yú mín
What is taken from the people is used for the people.

Example:

我們取道上海前往東京。
Wǒmen qǔdào Shànghǎi qiánwǎng Dōngjīng.
We go to Tokyo via Shanghai.

一個漢字一幅畫

qù

(go; leave)

去

去 is comprised of two parts in the oracle bones: the upper part was originally a person (大), and the lower part was a mouth (ㅂ or ∪). This indicated that a person had left the mouth of a cave. So the original meaning of 去 is "to leave", but it has also been extended to mean "to go" or "to remove" etc.

去處	qùchù	place to go
去路	qùlù	outlet
去年	qùnián	last year
去世	qùshì	(of grown-up people) die; pass away
去向	qùxiàng	the direction in which sb. or sth. has gone
去污粉	qùwūfěn	household cleanser

去粗取精
qù cū qǔ jīng
discard the dross and select the essential

去偽存真
qù wěi cún zhēn
eliminate the false and retain the true

去惡從善
qù è cóng shàn
exterminate the evil and follow the good

去邪歸正
qù xié guī zhèng
depart from the evil ways and return to good ways

何去何從
hé qù hé cóng
decide on what path to follow

Example:

這是一個極好的避暑去處。
Zhè shì yíge jíhǎo de bìshǔ qù chù.
This is a very nice place for summer.

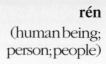

rén
(human being;
person; people)

The earliest known pictographs of this very important character show the figure of a person in profile—head, hands, and legs (勹). This evolved stylistically towards the present form, two strokes that appear to show the legs in frontal view. The original pictographs may suggest an insight into man's evolution from the anthropoids—or even earlier forms of life—and this, in turn, suggests a link with prehistoric knowledge now all but lost to us.

人類	rénlèi	humanity
人民	rénmín	people
人生	rénshēng	life
人格	réngé	personality
人權	rénquán	human rights
人性	rénxìng	human nature

Each Character A Picture the Chinese Written Language

人情世故
rén qíng shì gù
worldly wisdom

人言可畏
rén yán kě wèi
Gossip is a fearful thing.

人去樓空
rén qù lóu kōng
The chamber is empty with the dear person has gone away.

人生幾何
rén shēng jǐ hé
How long is a man's life?

人無遠慮，必有近憂
rén wú yuǎn lǜ, bì yǒu jìn yōu
A person who has no anxious thoughts for the future will find trouble right at hand.

Example:

三人行必有吾師焉。(**from Confucius**)
Sān rén xíng bì yǒu wǔ shī yān.
Three people being together, there must be one who can be my teacher.

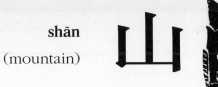

shān

(mountain)

The earlier form is clearly a pictographic representation of three peaks standing side by side (Ⱳ) , creating the form and shape of a large mountain. Later, for the sake of convenience in writing, the peaks developed into single strokes.

山城	shānchéng	mountain city
山頂	shāndǐng	the summit of the mountain
山洞	shāndòng	cave
山岡	shāngǎng	low hill
山谷	shāngǔ	mountain valley
山嶺	shānlǐng	mountain ridge
山區	shānqū	mountainous area

山盟海誓
shān méng hǎi shì
(make) a solemn pledge of love

山明水秀
shān míng shuǐ xiù
green hills and clear waters

i.e., picturesque scenery

山南海北
shān nán hái běi
south of the mountains and north of the seas

i.e., all over the land; far and wide

山外有山，天外有天
shān wài yǒu shān, tiān wài yǒu tiān
There are mountains beyond mountains, and heavens beyond heavens.

i.e., The grass is always greener on the other side of fence.

山窮水盡疑無路，柳暗花明又一村
shān qióng shuǐ jìn yí wú lù, liǔ àn huā míng yòu yì cūn
When the mountains and rivers come to an end and one would think there is no path, the shady willows and bright blossoms bring him to another village.

Example:

中國和緬甸是山水相連的友好鄰國。
Zhōngguó hé Miǎndiàn shì shān shuǐ xiāng lián de yóu hǎo líng guó.
China and Burma are linked by mountains and rivers.

一個漢字一幅畫

shàng

(above; upper)

The form of 上 on the oracle bones was represented as two horizontal lines(二); the one below indicates the "horizon" and the one above indicates "above the horizon". Later the form of the upper horizontal line was stylized a little (上), and the meaning of the character has also become clearer.

上班	shàngbān	go to work
上面	shàngmian	above; on the top of
上賓	shàngbīn	distinguished guest
上層	shàngcéng	upper strata; upper levels
上當	shàngdàng	be taken in; be fooled
上等	shàngděng	first-class; superior
上帝	shàngdì	God
上古	shànggǔ	ancient times
上級	shàngjí	higher authorities
上街	shàngjiē	go into the street
上課	shàngkè	attend class
上司	shàngsi	superior; boss

上行下效
shàng xíng xià xiào
What those above do, those below will follow.
i.e., People follow the examples of their superiors.

上達下情
shàng dá xià qíng
make the situation at the lower level known to the higher authorities

上刀山，下火海
shàng dāo shān, xià huó hǎi
climb a mountain of swords or plunge into a sea of flames
i.e., undergo the most severe trials

上樑不正下樑歪
shàng liáng bú zhèng xià liáng wāi
If the upper beams are not in the right position (straight), the lower ones are out of plumb (will go aslant).
i.e., When those above behave unworthily, those below will do the same.

上氣不接下氣
shàng qì bù jiē xià qì
i.e., be out (short) of breath

上天無路，入地無門
shàng tiān wú lù, rù dì wú mén
There is no road to the heaven and no door into the earth.
i.e., at the end of the hope

上無古人，下無來者
shàng wú gǔ rén, xià wú lái zhě
no ancients in the past, no posterity to come

Example:

時間到了，快上飛機吧！
Shíjiān dào le, kuài shàng fēijī ba!
It's time to get on the plane!

一個漢字一幅畫

shǎo

(less; few; little)

少

The character 少 is a combination of (丷) "small" and (丿) which indicates cutting something smaller. As it is smaller, it is of course less. Another saying is that the original form of the character was four dots which represented sand; later the third dot became longer, seeming to imply the location of the sand.

少刻	shǎokè	after a little while
少量	shǎoliàng	a small amount
少數	shǎoshù	small number; minority
少許	sháoxǔ	a little
少陪	shǎopéi	if you'll excuse me
少不得	shǎo bù dé	cannot do without
少數民族	shǎoshù mínzú	national minority

少見多怪
shǎo jiàn duō guài
comment excitedly on a commonplace thing
i.e., out of ignorance or inexperience

少說為妙
shǎo shuō wéi miào
The less said the better.

少智為福
shǎo zhì wéi fú
Ignorance is bliss.

少安無躁
shǎo ān wú zào
don't be impatient, wait for a while

少食多餐
shǎo shí duō cān
have more meals a day but less food at each

Example:

最近我很少見到他。
Zuìjìn wǒ hén shǎo jiàn dào tā.
I have seen very little of him recently.

一 個 漢 字 一 幅 畫

shēn

(body)

身

This character originally meant "pregnant", and depicted a human figure with a prominent belly and one leg thrust forward for support and balance (🖎). The modern form means the "human body".

身邊	shēnbiān	at (or by) one's side
身材	shēncái	figure
身長	shēncháng	height (of a person)
身價	shēnjià	social status
身軀	shēnqū	body; stature
身世	shēnshì	life experience
身手	shēnshǒu	skill
身体	shēntǐ	body
身心	shēnxīn	body and mind

身不由己
shēn bù yóu jǐ
involuntarily

身經百戰
shēn jīng bǎi zhàn
have fought a hundred battles

身臨其境
shēn lín qí jìng
be personally on the scene

身體力行
shēn tǐ lì xíng
earnestly practise what one advocates

身先士卒
shēn xiān shì zú
lead one's men in a charge

Example:

這套衣服很合身。
Zhèi tào yīfu hěn héshēn.
This suit fits (the body) perfectly.

133

一 個 漢 字 一 幅 畫

shēng

(grow)

生

The original character 生 is a very vivid pictographic representation of a growing seedling (Ψ) : the horizontal stroke at the bottom of the character indicates the land; on the land a small seedling appears to have just broken through the soil, growing with vitality. Later the horizontal stroke turned into (土) "soil", and the seedling became like the shoot of a tree; finally the "tree" lost its shape and the character has became like the one we see today. The original meaning of 生 is precisely the growth of grass or a tree; later it was extended to mean "alive" or "living"; it was also borrowed to mean "raw".

生詞	shēngcí	new word
生產	shēngchǎn	produce
生存	shēngcún	live; exist
生動	shēngdòng	lively
生活	shēnghuó	life
生理	shēnglǐ	physiology
生日	shēngrì	birthday

生不逢時
shēng bù féng shí
be born at a wrong time

生老病死
shēng lǎo bìng sǐ
birth, age, illness and death

生靈塗炭
shēng líng tú tàn
plunge the people into misery and suffering

生龍活虎
shēng lóng huó hǔ
doughty as a dragon and lively as a tiger
i.e., full of vim and vigor

生米煮成熟飯
shēng mǐ zhǔ chéng shú fàn
The rice is cooked.
i.e., What's done can't be undone.

生死之交
shēng sǐ zhī jiāo
friendship between the two sharing each other's fate

生有涯而知無限
shēng yǒu yá ér zhī wú xiàn
Life is limited, but knowledge is limitless.

生於憂患，死於安樂
shēng yú yōu huàn, sǐ yú ān lè
Misery and affliction make a man diligent, and so he lives; peace and happiness make a man lazy, and so he perishes.

Example:

我生在香港，長在香港。
Wǒ shēng zài Xiānggǎng, zhǎng zài Xiānggǎng.
I was born in Hong Kong and grew up in Hong Kong.

shēng

(sound)

聲

The upper left hand part of this character is in the shape of a inverted bell ( ); to the right is a hand holding a bell stick ( ) while in the middle is an ear ( ) and a mouth ( ). Therfore the whole picture indicates that words and music entering the ears is "sound". Later the mouth was removed from this character and the current form resulted.

聲波	shēngbō	sound wave
聲調	shēngdiào	tone
聲名	shēngmíng	reputation
聲明	shēngmíng	state; declare
聲勢	shēngshì	impetus
聲望	shēngwàng	popularity
聲響	shēngxiǎng	sound; noise
聲言	shēngyán	profess
聲音	shēngyīn	sound; voice
聲譽	shēngyù	reputation; fame

Each Character A Picture the Chinese Written Language

聲東擊西
shēng dōng jī xī
feint to the east but attack in the west

聲淚俱下
shēng lèi jù xià
loud and bitter weeping

聲名赫赫
shēng míng hè hè
to have awe-inspiring fame

聲名狼籍
shēng míng láng jí
to cause sb.to fall into discredit

聲色俱厲
shēng sè jù lì
stern in voice and countenance

聲勢浩大
shēng shì hào dà
great in strength and impetus

Example:

我們聽到遠處有各種奇怪的聲音。
Wǒmen tīngdào yuǎnchù yǒu gèzhǒng qíguài de shēngyīn.
We heard strange sounds in the distance.

一 個 漢 字 一 幅 畫

shuāng

(two; twin; both; dual)

The original form of the character 雙 is a complex one, above which depicts two "birds" (羅) with their beaks turned to the left, sitting on a "right hand"(ㄟ). This combination indicates one hand catching two birds, which suggests the concept of "a pair".

雙重	shuāngchóng	double
雙方	shuāngfāng	both side
雙幅	shuāngfú	double width
雙關	shuāngguān	having a double meaning
雙親	shuāngqīn	father and mother
雙手	shuāngshǒu	both hands
雙數	shuāngshù	even numbers
雙雙	shuāngshuāng	in pairs
雙喜	shuāngxǐ	double happiness

雙雙對對
shuāng shuāng duì duì
in pairs and couples
雙宿雙飛
shuāng sù shuāng fēi
always keep each other's company
雙喜臨門
shuāng xǐ lín mén
A double blessing has descended upon the house.
雙管齊下
shuāng guǎn qí xià
paint a picture with two brushes at the same time
i.e., work along both lines

Example:

這布是單幅還是雙幅？
Zhè bù shì dānfú hái shì shuāngfú?
Is this cloth single or double width?

一 個 漢 字 一 幅 畫

shuǐ

(water)

水

The original character 水 was formed by a stream in the middle ( ) with dots on both sides ( ) representing drops of water. In the inscriptions on oracle bones, the number of "drops" of water varied, but later it was fixed as two for each side. Gradually it developed to the form we see today. 水 as a radical is usually written as (氵). Chinese characters with this radical mostly have something to do with water.

水兵	**shuǐbīng**	**seamam**
水彩	**shuícǎi**	**watercolour**
水產	**shuíchǎn**	**aquatic product**
水池	**shuǐchí**	**pool; pond**
水電	**shuǐdiàn**	**water and electricity**
水管	**shuíguǎn**	**waterpipe**
水果	**shuíguǒ**	**fruit**
水晶	**shuǐjīng**	**crystal**
水力	**shuǐlì**	**waterpower**

水到渠成
shuǐ dào jú chéng
When water flows, a channel is formed.

i.e., When conditions are ripe, success will come.

水滴石穿
shuǐ dī shí chuān
Dripping water wears through rock.

i.e., constant effort brings success

水底撈月
shuí dǐ lāo yuè
dredge the moon out from the bottom of the water

水火不容
shuí huǒ bù róng
no intercourse between water and fire

水落石出
shuǐ luò shí chū
When the water subsides the rocks emerge

i.e., The whole thing comes to light.

水漲船高
shuí zhǎng chuán gāo
When the river rises the boat goes up.

水有源，樹有根
shuǐ yǒu yuán, shù yǒu gēn
Every river has its source and every tree has its roots.

i.e., Everything has its origin.

Example:

天氣熱，多喝點兒水。
Tiānqì rè, duō hē diǎnr shuǐ.
It's very hot, you should drink more water.

sī

(silk)

絲

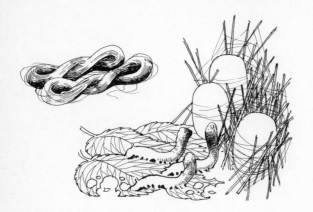

This was a pictogram of two reels of silk threads tied together (絲), meaning cocoon silk. Because silk thread is very fine and thin, 絲 was later used to describe things that were very delicate. Moreover, 絲 also meant string instruments in ancient China, and 竹 (zhú: bamboo) meant woodwind instruments.

絲綢	sīchóu	silk cloth
絲帶	sīdài	silk ribbon
絲瓜	sīguā	fruit of loofah
絲光	sīguāng	the silky luster of mercerized cotton fabrics
絲毫	sīháo	the slightest amount or degree
絲綿	sīmián	silk floss
絲絨	sīróng	velvet
絲線	sīxiàn	silk thread
絲織品	sīzhìpǐn	silk fabrics
絲竹	sīzhú	traditional stringed and woodwind instruments; music

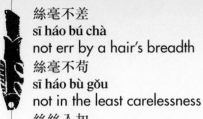

絲毫不差
sī háo bú chà
not err by a hair's breadth

絲毫不苟
sī háo bù gǒu
not in the least carelessness

絲絲入扣
sī sī rù kòu
with meticulous care and flawless artistry

絲竹管弦
sī zhú guǎn xián
music of string and flute

絲恩髮怨
sī ēn fà yuàn
gratitude for the slightest favour received or grudge against the slightest wrong done.

Example:

絲綢之路值得一遊。
Sīchóu zhī lù zhíde yì yóu.
It is worthwhile to take a trip to the Silk Road.

tiān

(sky; heaven)

天

人　大　天

(人) represented the form of man, but it was only a body without the head. Then a "head" was added above the space of the body and it became (夨). So originally, 天 indicated "the head" of a man's body. At the beginning this "head" was as round as a ball, but later it gradually became flat, and finally it became a horizontal stroke like in the modern version. As the growing light of the sky brings in the dawn of the day, 天 also came to mean "day".

天地	tiāndì	heaven and earth
天才	tiāncái	genius
天空	tiānkōng	the sky
天亮	tiānliàng	daybreak; dawn
天堂	tiāntáng	paradise
天氣	tiānqì	weather
天然	tiānrán	natural
天生	tiānshēng	born; inborn

天長地久
tiān cháng dì jiǔ
as long as the heaven and the earth endure

天從人願
tiān cóng rén yuàn
Heaven follows man's wish.

天馬行空
tiān mǎ xíng kōng
A heavenly steed soaring across the skies.

i.e., a powerful and unconstrained style

天網恢恢，疏而不漏
tiān wǎng huī huī, shū ér bú lòu
The net of heaven has large meshes, but it lets nothing through.

i.e., Justice has long arms.

天下本無事，庸人自造之
tiān xià běn wú shì, yōng rén zì zào zhī
There is nothing wrong under heaven originally, the philistine worries about troubles of his own imagination.

天下烏鴉一般黑
tiān xià wū yā yì bān hēi
All crows under heaven are black.

天下無難事，只怕有心人
tiān xià wú nán shì, zhǐ pà yǒu xīn rén
All difficulties on the earth can be overcome if men but to give their minds to it.

i.e., Where there is a will, there is a way.

Example:

我在北京獃了三天。
Wǒ zài Běijīng dāile sān tiān.
I have stayed in Beijing for three days.

一個漢字一幅畫

tǔ

(soil; earth)

土

土 is a pictograph which shows a pile of soil in a field (𝟃). The upper part represents the soil and the lower part represents the field.

土產	túchǎn	local product
土地	tǔdì	land
土話	tǔhuà	local dialect
土木	tǔmù	construction
土壤	túrǎng	soil
土人	tǔrén	native
土音	tǔyīn	local accent
土著	tǔzhù	original inhabitants
土皇帝	tǔhuángdì	local despot

土崩瓦解
tǔ bēng wá jiě
fall apart

土豪劣紳
tǔ háo liè shēn
local tyrants and evil gentry

土生土長
tǔ shēng tú zhǎng
locally born and bred

土洋結合
tǔ yáng jié hé
combine indigenous and foreign methods

Example:

這兒的土壤很肥沃。
Zhèr'de túrǎng hěn féiwò.
The soil here is very fertile.

(king)

王

王 is formed by adding a horizontal stroke under the "person"(大) and another horizontal stroke above the "person" (天). As the two "legs" of the "person" 大 close together then they become a vertical stroke. It is said that the three horizontal strokes represent the heaven, the earth, and the person. The person who could join the three together is the king.

王朝	wángcháo	imperial court; dynasty
王儲	wángchǔ	crown prince
王法	wángfǎ	the law of the land
王宮	wánggōng	palace
王冠	wángguān	imperial crown; royal crown
王國	wángguó	kingdom
王侯	wánghóu	princes and marquises
王后	wánghòu	queen; queen consort
王室	wángshì	royal family
王位	wángwèi	throne
王子	wángzǐ	prince

Each Character A Picture the Chinese Written Language

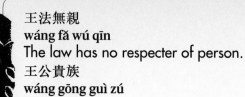

王法無親
wáng fǎ wú qīn
The law has no respecter of person.

王公貴族
wáng gōng guì zú
the nobility

王者以民為天
wáng zhě yǐ mín wéi tiān
A king's life depends upon the people.

王子犯法，與民同罪
wángzǐ fànfǎ, yǔ mín tóng zuì
If a prince violates the law, he must be punished like an ordinary person.

Example:

中國有句諺語："成者為王，敗者為寇。"
Zhōngguó yǒu jù yànyǔ: "Chéng zhě wéi wáng, bài zhě wéi kòu."
This is a Chinese idiom saying: "The one who wins becomes a king and the one who lose becomes a bandit."

xī

(west) 西

The original form of 西 was drawn as a bird's nest ( ) in the oracle bones, but it developed into a more complicated form later with the addition of a curve above the nest ( ) representing a bird. This change makes the meaning of this character clearer: when the sun falls to the west, birds return to their nests; and that is the origin of the meaning of this character for 西 "west".

西方	xīfāng	the west
西餐	xīcān	Western style food
西風	xīfēng	west wind
西瓜	xīguā	watermelon
西南	xīnán	southwest
西歐	Xī'ōu	Western Europe
西天	xītiān	Western Paradise
西洋	xīyáng	the Western world
西藥	xīyào	Western medicine
西裝	xīzhuāng	Western-style clothes

西方淨土
xī fāng jìng tǔ
the heavenly paradise (of Buddhism)
i.e., The happy land in the west.

西風殘照
xī fēng cán zhào
a setting sun in the west wind

西風落葉
xī fēng luò yè
the west wind and fallen leaves

i.e., an autumn scene

西窗剪燭
xī chuāng jiǎn zhú
The happy reunion of friends chatting together later at night.

Example:

香港是個東西文化交匯的城市。
Xiānggǎng shì ge dōng xī wénhuà jiāohuì de chéngshì.
Hong Kong is a city with a blending culture of East and West.

xí

(learn)

習

This is a very interesting character. The perceptive reader may have already noticed that the upper part of this character is a (⺳) which we have learned means "feathers" or "wings". The lower part of the character, "self" (⊙) is what relates the feathers to learning. The two parts together means a bird trying to learn how to fly by itself and thus derives the meaning of "learn".

習見	xíjiàn	(of things) commonly seen
習氣	xíqì	bad habit
習俗	xísú	custom
習題	xítí	exercises (in school work)
習性	xíxìng	habits and characteristics
習用	xíyòng	habitually use
溫習	wēnxí	review

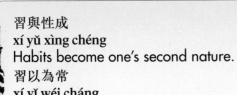

習與性成
xí yǔ xìng chéng
Habits become one's second nature.

習以為常
xí yǐ wéi cháng
be used to sth.

習非成是
xí fēi chéng shì
Accept what is wrong as right as one grows accustomed to it.

習焉不察
xí yān bù chá
Too accustomed to something to call it in question.

Example:

小王在溫習功課。
Xiǎo wáng zài wēnxí gōngkè.
Xiao Wang is reviewing his lessons.

一 個 漢 字 一 幅 畫

xǐ

(happy; joy)

喜

In the oracle bones, this character is comprised of two parts: the upper part means "drum" (the original form of 鼓 drum) and the lower part means mouth (⊌) . "Drum" indicates "happy" or "joyful" feelings, and the "mouth" is a symbol of happy or joyful voices. So "happy", " joyful" and "pleased" are the original meanings of this character. Later it was also extended to mean "to like" or "to be fond of", and also "pregnancy".

喜愛	xǐʾài	like; be fond of
喜歡	xǐhuān	like; be fond of
喜酒	xújiǔ	the wine drunk at a wedding
喜劇	xǐjù	comedy
喜慶	xǐqìng	joyous
喜事	xǐshì	happy event; wedding
喜訊	xǐxùn	happy news
喜悦	xǐyuè	happy; joyous
喜衝衝	xǐ chōng chōng	look exhilarated

Each Character A Picture the Chinese Written Language

喜出望外
xǐ chū wàng wài
be overjoyed
喜怒不形於色
xǐ nù bù xíng yú sè
not show joy or anger on one's face
喜氣洋洋
xǐ qì yáng yáng
full of joy
喜從天降
xǐ cóng tiān jiàng
unexpected good news comes from the sky
喜新厭舊
xǐ xīn yàn jiù
love the new and loathe the old

Example:

鄭先生喜歡在大海裡游泳。
Zhèng xiānsheng xǐhuan zài dàháilǐ yóuyǒng.
Mr. Zheng likes to swim in the sea.

一個漢字一幅畫

xiān

(before; first)

先

A man facing left with a footprint above his head (㞢), expressing the idea of "walking ahead". This is the original meaning of 先. Later the meaning was extended to include "before", "earlier" or "first".

先鋒	xiānfēng	the vanguard
先進	xiānjìn	advanced
先例	xiānlì	precedent
先驅	xiānqū	pioneer; forerunner
先生	xiānsheng	mister; gentleman; sir
先天	xiāntiān	congenital; inborn

先入為主
xiān rù wéi zhǔ
First impressions are lasting impressions.
先聲奪人
xiān shēng duó rén
forestall one's opponent by a show of strength
先睹為快
xiān dǔ wéi kuài
consider it a pleasure to be among the first to read (see) sth.
先禮後兵
xiān lǐ hòu bīng
trying courteous means before resorting to force
先天下之憂而憂，後天下之樂而樂
xiān tiān xià zhī yōu ér yōu, hòu tiān xià zhī lè ér lè
A leader should worry ahead of the people and enjoy the fruits after the people.

Example:

他先去北京，再去上海。
Tā xiān qù Běijīng, zài qù Shànghǎi.
He will go to Beijing first and then go to Shanghai.

xiao

(small)

小

The character 小 in the oracle bones is formed by three short verticals (ₗ¦ₗ). The vertical in the middle depicts a small object and the other two on either side are the halves of a separated 八, which means "divide" as we know. When something being divided it naturally becomes "small".

小報	xiǎobào	tabloid
小吃	xiǎochī	snack; refreshment
小丑	xiáochǒu	clown; buffoon
小販	xiǎofàn	hawker
小費	xiǎofèi	tip
小姐	xiáojiě	Miss; young lady
小事	xiǎoshì	petty thing
小説	xiǎoshuō	novel; fiction
小老婆	xiáolǎo po	concubine
小心	xiǎoxīn	take care; be careful
小學	xiǎoxué	primary school
小算盤	xiǎosuànpan	selfish calculation

158

小恩小惠
xiǎo ēn xiǎo huì
petty favours

小巫見大巫
xiǎowū jiàn dàwū
seem like a pigmy compared with the devil

小不忍則亂大謀
xiǎo bù rěn zé luàn dà móu
A little impatience spoils great plans.

小患不治成大災
xiǎo huàn bú zhì chéng dà zāi
A small leak can sink a great ship.

Example:

我買了一份小禮物給我女兒。
Wǒ mǎi le yífèn xiáolǐwù géi wǒ nǚér.
I bought a small gift for my daughter.

xiào

(filial piety)

孝

The original shape of 孝 is also very interesting. Look at the upper part of the character you will find an old man with hunchback and long hair (耂) and the lower part is a child (𡥀) as we already know. The old man has put his hand on the head of the child, and the child is supporting him while walking (孝). What the character means is exactly what it shows: "filial piety towards old people" 孝 , which is one of the most important element in traditional Chinese culture.

孝敬	xiàojìng	give presents (to one's elders or superiors)
孝顺	xiàoshùn	show filial obedience
孝子	xiàozǐ	dutiful son
带孝	dàixiào	in mourning
孝道	xiàodáo	filial piety

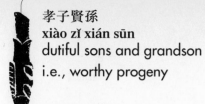

孝子賢孫
xiào zǐ xián sūn
dutiful sons and grandson
i.e., worthy progeny

Example:

中國人很重視孝道。
Zhōngguó rén hěn zhòngshì xiàodào.
Chinese emphasize a lot on filial piety.

xīn

(heart; feeling; center)

心

This character is a primitive anatomical representation of a heart. The original meaning of 心 is just for "the heart"; it was also extended to mean "mind" or "feelings". As the ancients thought that the heart was in the middle of the chest, it has also been extended to mean "center" or "core".

心愛	xīn'ài	love; treasure
心地	xīndì	a person's character; moral nature
心肝	xīngān	conscience
心理	xīnlǐ	psychology
心情	xīnqíng	mood
心事	xīnshì	a load on one's mind; worry
心思	xīnsī	thought; idea
心願	xīnyuàn	cherished desire; wish

心不在焉
xīn bú zài yān
absent-minded

心高氣傲
xīn gāo qì ào
proud and arrogant

心狠手辣
xīn hěn shǒu là
hard-hearted and cruel

心灰意懶
xīn huī yì lǎn
One's heart sinks.

心曠神怡
xīn kuàng shén yí
free of mind, happy of heart

心猿意馬
xīn yuán yì mǎ
One's heart is agile as an ape and one's thoughts swift as a horse.

心照不宣
xīn zhào bù xuān
understand each other without anything being spelt (out)

心有餘而力不足
xīn yǒu yú ér lì bù zú
one's ability falls short of one's wish

心像平原走馬，易放難收
xīn xiàng píng yuán zóu mǎ, yì fàng nán shōu
The mind is like a horse on the plain, easy to let go but difficult to stop.

Example:

他人在這兒，心卻不在。
Tā rén zài zhèr, xīn què búzài.
He himself is here, but his thoughts are at home.

一個漢字一幅畫

xìn
(confidence; believe;
letter; correspondence)

信

The character 信 is an associative compound comprised of 人 (rén: person) on the left and 言 (yán: speech/word) on the right, signifying that the words of a person should be true. So the original meaning of this character is "words being true and honest"; it has also been extended to mean "confidence", "to believe", and "letter" etc.

信貸	xìndài	credit
信封	xìnfēng	envelope
信服	xìnfú	completely accept
信奉	xìnfèng	believe in
信號	xìnhào	signal
信件	xìnjiàn	mail, letters
信念	xìnniàn	belief; faith
信任	xìnrèn	trust
信息	xìnxī	information
信箱	xìnxiāng	letter box
信心	xìnxīn	confidence

Each Character A Picture the Chinese Written Language

信誓旦旦
xìn shī dàn dàn
pledge in all sincerity and seriousness

信賞必罰
xìn shǎng bì fá
due rewards and punishments will be meted out without fail

信口雌黃
xìn kǒu cī huáng
wag one's tongue too freely

i.e., make irresponsible remarks.

信口開河
xìn kǒu kāi hé
wag one's tongue too freely

i.e., talk nonsense

信守諾言
xìn shǒu nuò yán
keep one's promise

Example:

他不是一個可以信賴的人。
Tā búshì yíge kéyǐ xìnlài de rén.
He's not the sort of man to be trusted.

xiū

(rest)

休 is a combination of (亻) and (木), picturing a person resting against a tree, signifying "rest" 休息 . From this original meaning, it was extended to mean "stop", as in "爭論不休" (zhēng lùn bù xiū: "argue without stop"). From "stop", it was borrowed to mean "don't", as in " 休要胡說 " (xiū yào hú shuō: "don't talk nonsense").

休假	xiūjià	have holiday
休息	xiūxi	have a rest; rest
休閒	xiūxián	lie fallow
休學	xiūxué	suspend one's schooling without losing one's status as a student
休養	xiūyǎng	recuperate
休戰	xiūzhàn	cease-fire

Each Character A Picture the Chinese Written Language

休養生息
xiū yǎng shēng xī
rest and build up strength

休棄前嫌
xiū qì qián xián
repudiate a previous grievance

休戚相關
xiū qì xiāng guān
mutually concerned in case of good or bad turn

爭論不休
zhēng lùn bù xiū
argue ceaselessly

休要自誇
xiū yào zì kuā
Don't talk big.

Example:

今天我休息。
Jīntiān wǒ xiūxi.
Today I'm off.

xuè

(blood)

血

The character 血 is represented by adding a horizontal stroke (•) on a vessel (皿) "ming" indicating what the vessel holds is blood. The original meaning of 血 was the blood used for sacrificial rites.

血管	xuèguǎn	blood vessel
血汗	xuèhàn	blood and sweat
血肉	xuèròu	flesh and blood
血色	xuèsè	redness of the skin
血統	xuètǒng	blood relationship
血型	xuèxíng	blood group; blood type
血壓	xuèyā	blood pressure
血液	xuèyè	blood
血緣	xuèyuán	ties of blood

血口噴人
xuè kǒu pēn rén
cast malicious words to injure sb.
血脈相通
xuè mài xiāng tōng
be of one blood
血氣方剛
xuè qì fāng gāng
full of sap
血肉相連
xuè ròu xiāng lián
be related by flesh and blood
血肉之軀
xuè ròu zhī qū
mortal flesh and blood
血比水濃，疏不間親
xuè bǐ shuǐ nóng, shú bù jiān qīn
Blood is thicker than water.

Example:

他受傷後流了很多血。
Tā shòu shāng hòu liú le hěn duō xuè (xiě).
He has lost a lot of blood since he was injured.

yán

(scorching)

炎

Two fires combined together, one atop the other, like flames licking the sky (炎), represents the idea of "a roaring fire." This is original meaning of 炎 . Then it was extended to mean "burn"; from "burn" it was also extended to mean "burning hot", as in " 赤日炎炎 " (chìrì yányán: "the scorching sun").

炎熱	yánrè	scorching; blazing
炎日	yánrì	scorching sun
炎夏	yánxià	hot summer
炎炎	yányán	scorching; blazing

炎黃子孫
yán huáng zǐ sūn
descendants of the Chinese nation
炎涼世態
yán liáng shì tài
the aspect of worldly affairs
炎附寒棄
yán fù hán qì
cleave to influential and wealthy persons and discard poor and mean ones.
赤日炎炎
zhi ri yán yán
the blazing sun

Example:

天氣炎熱，小心中暑。
Tiānqì yánrè, xiǎoxīn zhòngshǔ.
The weather is scorching. Be careful not to get sunstroke.

yán
(speech; word;
to say)

言

Originally the bottom part of the character was a drawing of a tongue ( ), and the vertical line above it represented the speech produced by the tongue. 言 can also be a radical. The characters using this radical have something to do with speech, language or morality.

言詞	yáncí	one's words
言和	yánhé	make peace
言論	yánlùn	opinion on public affairs
言談	yántán	the way one speaks or what he says
言行	yánxíng	words and deeds
言語	yányǔ	spoken language

言傳身教
yán chuán shēn jiào
teach by words and lead by example
i.e., to practise what you preach

言出必行
yán chū bì xíng
suit the action to the word

言為心聲
yán wéi xīn shēng
Words are the voice of the mind.

言外之意
yán wài zhī yì
what one actually meant

言必信，行必果
yán bì xìn, xíng bì guǒ
always be true in word and resolute in deed.

Example:

如果你老是食言，就沒有人會再相信你。
Rúguǒ nǐ lǎo shì shí yán, jiù méi yǒu rén huì zài xiāngxìn nǐ.
If you always break your promises, no one will trust you anymore.

yáng

(sheep)

羊

(♈) pictures the frontal view of a sheep: two horns and a triangle towards the bottom representing the mouth. Later the triangle was divided into one vertical stroke and three horizontal strokes; and this is how we write the character today.

羊羔	yánggāo	lamb
羊倌	yángguān	shepherd
羊毫	yánghóo	writing brush made of goat's hair
羊圈	yángjuàn	sheepfold
羊毛	yángmáo	sheep's wool
羊皮	yángpí	sheepskin
羊絨	yángróng	cashmere
羊肉	yángròu	mutton

Each Character A Picture the Chinese Written Language

羊質虎皮
yáng zhì hǔ pí
a sheep's body in a tiger's skin
羊落虎口
yáng luò hú kǒu
a sheep fallen into the tiger's mouth
羊入狼群
yáng rù láng qún
a sheep entering a pack of wolves
羊群裡頭出駱駝
yáng qún lǐ tou chū luòtuo
stand out like a camel in a flock of sheep
羊肉不曾吃，空惹一身膻
yáng ròu bù céng chī, kōng rě yì shēn shān
not having eaten the mutton but instead invited a strong smell all of the body

i.e., not having got any advantage but invited trouble
羊毛出在羊身上
yáng máo chū zài yáng shēn shàng
After all, the wool still comes from the sheep's back.

i.e., In the long turn, whatever you are given, you pay for.

Example:

北京的涮羊肉很出名。
Běijīng de shuànyángròu hěn chūmíng.
The instant-boiled mutton in Beijing is very well-known.

一個漢字一幅畫

yǎng
(raise)

養

The original form of (養) was a combination with (羊) "sheep" on the left and a right hand (又) with a vertical strokes on the right. This suggests putting a sheep to pasture with a hand holding a whip. As "to raise" means "to give food", so, later the form was changed with "whip" being replaced by 食 (food) below.

養病	yǎngbìng	recuperate
養分	yǎngfèn	nutrient
養活	yǎnghuo	support; feed
養料	yǎngliào	nutriment
養神	yǎngshén	rest and attain mental tranquility
養生	yǎngshēng	preserve one's health
養育	yǎngyù	bring up
養魚池	yǎngyúchí	fishpond

養而不教
yǎng ér bú jiào
bear the children without educating them

養兒防老
yǎng ér fáng lǎo
raise children to provide against old age

養虎為患
yáng hǔ wéi huàn
nourish a tiger to source of trouble in future

養精蓄銳
yǎng jīng xù ruì
conserve one's strength and store up energy

養老送終
yáng lǎo sòng zhōng
provide for the aged parent(s) and attend upon their funeral(s)

養性修身
yǎng xìng xiū shēn
promote conduct and practise ethics

養尊處優
yǎng zūn chù yōu
enjoy in a high position and live in ease and comfort

養兵千日，用於一朝
yǎng bīng qiān rì, yòng yú yì zhāo
Troops are kept a thousand days to be used on one day.

Example:

我們要感激父母的養育之恩。
Wǒmen yào gǎnjī fù mǔ de yǎng yù zhī ēn.
We must gratitude to our parents for their love and care from our childhood.

一個漢字一幅畫

yè
(night)

夜

This character originated from the pictograph (夜), which is a drawing of a person standing straight. By adding a dot (丶) under the right arm of the person, means underarm. Then by putting a (刀) " 月 yuè: the moon" under the left arm of the person, means the moon has risen to the height of a person's underarm. This indicates that nighttime has arrived. Therefore (夜) means "night". After thousands of years, (夜) has changed to " 夜 ", but the meaning still remains.

夜半	yèbàn	midnight
夜車	yèchē	night train
夜航	yèháng	night flight or navigation
夜間	yèjiān	at night
夜幕	yèmù	curtain of night
夜色	yèsè	the dim light of night
夜校	yèxiào	evening
夜宵	yèxiāo	food taken late at night
夜總會	yèzǒnghuì	night club

Each Character A Picture the Chinese Written Language

夜以繼日
yè yǐ jì rì
day and night

夜不閉戶
yè bú bì hù
doors were not closed at night

夜闌人靜
yè lán rén jìng
in the still of night

夜郎自大
yè láng zì dà
as cheekly as Yelang (chief), who thinks himself the equal of the Son of Heaven

夜長夢多
yè cháng mèng duō
A long night gives rise to many dreams. .
i.e., Heaven knows what may happen all this long while.

夜蛾赴火
yè é fù huǒ
A moth flying into the fire.
i.e., seek one's own doom

Example:

香港的夜景非常迷人。
Xiānggǎng de yèjǐng fēicháng mírén.
The night scene of Hong Kong is very charming.

一 個 漢 字 一 幅 畫

yī
(clothes)
衣

The shape of this character resembles that of an ancient Chinese-style shirt (衣). The (∧) portion looks like the collar and two sleeves, and the (ⴣ) part of the character represents the part of the shirt which flaps over from left to right. Unfortunately, the 衣 nowadays has lost most of its interesting resemblance to the Chinese-style shirt. As the pictogram suggests, the character 衣 originally meant "shirt", but later generalizations extended its meaning to include clothes of all kinds.

衣服	yīfu	clothing; clothes
衣櫥	yīchú	wardrobe
衣冠	yīguān	hat and clothes
衣架	yījià	coat hanger
衣料	yīliào	material for clothing
衣物	yīwù	clothing and other articles of daily use
衣箱	yīxiāng	suitcase
衣著	yīzhuó	clothing, headgear and footwear

衣冠楚楚
yī guān chú chǔ
be dressed like a gentleman

衣冠禽獸
yī guān qín shòu
A beast in human clothing.

i.e., A well dressed man of beastly temper.

衣食住行
yī shí zhù xíng
clothing, food, shelter and transportation

i.e., basic necessities of life

衣不如新，人不如故
yī bù rú xīn, rén bù rú gù
For clothes newer is better, for friends older is better.

衣食足，然後知榮辱
yī shí zú, rán hòu zhī róng rǔ
Well fed, well bred.

衣沾不足惜，但使願無違
yī zhān bù zú xī, dàn shǐ yuàn wú wéi
If I could follow my wish it would not matter if my clothes get soaked.

慈母手中線，遊子身上衣
cí mǔ shǒu zhōng xiàn, yóu zǐ shēn shàng yī
Through a kind mother's hands passed the thread, that made the clothes I journeying wear.

Example:

中國有句古話：衣食足，然後知榮辱。
Zhōngguó yǒu jù gǔ huà, yī shí zú, rán hòu zhī róng rǔ.
There is an old saying in Chinese: Well fed, well bred.

yǒu 友

(friend; friendship)

"Two right hands" close together ( ) in the inscriptions on oracle bones gives us the sense of two people with clasping each other's right hands to show their friendship; the persons performing this action are, of course "friends". So "friend" is precisely what this character originally meant. Later, for the convenience of writing, the form was changed to have one hand above the other, and that is the modern version we see today.

友愛	yǒu'ài	friendly affection
友邦	yǒubāng	friendly nation
友好	yóuhǎo	friendly
友情	yǒuqíng	friendly sentiment
友人	yǒurén	friend
友誼	yǒuyì	friendship

良師益友
liáng shī yì yǒu
good teacher and helpful friend

狐朋狗友
hú péng góu yǒu
bad friends

酒肉朋友
jiǔ ròu péng yǒu
wine and meat friends

i.e., friends in prosperity

友愛之誼
yǒu ài zhī yì
the friendliness of brothers

友好條約
yóu hǎo tiáo yuē
treaty of friendship

Example:

你真是我的良師益友。
Nǐ zhēn shì wǒ de liáng shī yì yǒu.
You are really my good teacher and helpful friend.

yǒu

(possess; have)

有

The ancient form of this character uses the character (⳽) on top of (𝐃) which itself is a form of the character 肉 (ròu: meat). As a whole, it depicts a right hand holding a piece of meat. To the ancients, possessing meat was felt akin to owning the entire world, therefore a right hand holding onto a piece of meat meant "have" or "possess". Gradually this character came to be used as an antonym to "無" (nothing, not possessing).

有功	yǒugōng	have rendered great service
有鬼	yóuguǐ	there is something fishy
有害	yǒuhài	harmful
有理	yóulǐ	reasonable
有利	yǒulì	advantageous
有限	yǒuxiàn	limited
有趣	yǒuqù	interesting; amusing
有效	yǒuxiào	efficacious

有口皆碑
yóu kǒu jié bēi
win universal praise

有利可圖
yǒu lì kě tú
have good prospects for gain

有備無患
yǒu bèi wú huàn
Where there is precaution, there is no danger.

有隙可乘
yǒu xī kě chéng
there is a crack to squeeze through

有奶便是娘
yóu nǎi biàn shì niáng
whoever suckles me is my mother

有眼不識泰山
yóu yǎn bù shí Tàishān
have eyes but fail to see Taishan Mountain

有則改之，無則加勉
yǒu zé gǎi zhī, wú zé jiā miǎn
correct mistakes if you have made any and guard against them if you have not

有志者事竟成
yǒu zhì zhě shì jìng chéng
Where there is a will there is a way.

Example:

我有一本漢英詞典。
Wó yǒu yìběn Hàn-Yīng cídiǎn.
I have a Chinese-English Dictionary.

yú
(fish)

魚

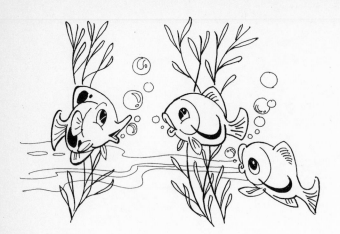

This character depicts the abdomen of a fish (魚), with the head upwards and the tail downwards. Later developments had the body all straightened into strokes, and the tail became four dots. The simplified version of the character 鱼 even changed the four dots to a horizontal line.

魚翅	yúchì	shark's fin
魚刺	yúcì	fishbone
魚竿	yúgān	fishing rod
魚肝油	yúgānyóu	cod-liver oil
魚鈎	yúgōu	fishhook
魚鱗	yúlín	fish scale
魚群	yúqún	shoal of fish
魚子	yúzǐ	roe
魚子醬	yúzǐjiàng	caviare

Each Character A Picture the Chinese Written Language

魚龍混雜
yú lóng hùn zá
Dragons and fishes jumbled together.
i.e., Good and bad people mixed up.
魚米之鄉
yú mǐ zhī xiāng
a land of fish and rice
i.e., a land of plenty
魚目混珠
yú mù hùn zhū
pass off fish eyes as pearls
i.e., pass off the sham as the genuine
魚水情深
yú shuǐ qíng shēn
be closed as fish and water
如魚得水
rú yú dé shuǐ
feel just like fish in water

Example:

中國的江南是魚米之鄉。
Zhōngguó de jiāng nán shì yú mǐ zhī xiāng.
The south of the Changjiang River is a land of plenty.

一個漢字一幅畫

yǔ
(rain)

雨

The original pictograph for (⫽) shows rain pouring down from clouds at a high altitude. As inscribed on the oracle bones, the horizontal stroke indicates the clouds, and the six short lines hanging down indicate the raindrops. Later, another horizontal stroke was added above, most probably to indicate the "sky".

雨點	yúdiǎn	raindrop
雨量	yǔliàng	rainfall
雨季	yǔjì	rainy season
雨傘	yúsǎn	umbrella
雨衣	yǔyī	raincoat
雨具	yǔjù	rain gear

雨過天晴
yǔ guò tiān qíng
the sun shines after the rain

雨後春筍
yǔ hòu chūn sǔn
spring up like bamboo shoots after a spring rain

大雨傾盆
dà yǔ qīn pén
The rain is pelting down.

春風化雨
chūn fēng huà yǔ
The life-giving spring breeze and rain.

i.e., The salutary influence of education.

Example:

外面在下雨，出去別忘了帶傘。
Wàimian zài xiàyǔ, chūqù bié wàng le dài sǎn.
It's raining outside. Don't forget to take the umbrella, when you go out.

一 個 漢 字 一 幅 畫

yù

(jade)

玉

In the oracle bones, this character is represented by a string tying three pieces of jade together. Ancient Chinese considered jade to be a treasure so they used strings to tie pieces of them together.

Because jade is a warm, soft and shiny gem stone, ancient people used the word to compliment beautiful and prestigious things, e.g. "玉顏" (yù yán: "beautiful face of a woman"), "玉女" (yù nǚ: "golden girl"), "玉成其事" (yù chéng qí shì: "to finish a task beautifully").

玉成	yùchéng	kindly help make a success of something
玉帶	yùdài	jade belt
玉雕	yùdiāo	jade carving
玉米	yùmǐ	maize
玉器	yùqì	jade article
玉色	yùsè	jade green
玉石	yùshí	jade

玉潔冰清
yù jié bīng qīng
as pure as jade and as clear as ice
玉石不分
yù shí bù fēn
make no distinction between jade and stone
玉液瓊漿
yù yè qióng jiāng
top-quality wine
玉不琢，不成器
yù bù zhuó, bù chéng qì
If jade is not polished, it can not be made into anything.
i.e., spare the rod and spoil the child

Example:

這是一件玉石飾物。
Zhèshì yíjiàn yùshí shìwù.
This is a jade ornament.

yuè

(moon; month) 月

As the moon spends more time in its waxing and waning stages than it does being full, the original pictograph 月 pictures a new moon hanging in the sky (〗). Later a vertical stroke was added inside the moon (𝔇) which was considered to indicate the bay tree as man imagined.

月份	yuèfèn	month
月光	yuèguāng	moonlight
月刊	yuèkān	monthly magazine
月曆	yuèlì	monthly calendar
月亮	yuèliang	the moon
月票	yuèpiào	monthly ticket
月台	yuètái	railway platform
月夜	yuèyè	moonlit night

月白風清
yuè bái fēng qīng
The moon is bright, the wind is soft.
月裡嫦娥
yuè lǐ cháng é
legendary fairy of the moon
月下花前
yuè xià huā qián
under the moonlight and in front of the flowers
i.e., the place for lovers
月下老人
yuè xià lǎo rén
The old man under the moon.
i.e., The God who unites persons in marriage.

Example:

一年有十二個月。
Yìnián yǒu shí'èr ge yuè.
There are twelve months in a year.

yún

(cloud)

雲

The original character for 雲 pictures a floating cloud curling up into the air(☁). The two short strokes on the upper part (⸗) form the ancient version of 上 "shàng", which represents the sky where the clouds are formed. Later, a 雨 was added on the top of the 云 to imply the relationship between "clouds" and "rain". Therefore, the original pictograph has turned into a pictophonetic character (雨 is pictographic; 云 is phonetic).

雲彩	yúncǎi	cloud
雲層	yúncén	cloud layer
雲煙	yúnyān	cloud and mist
雲海	yúnhǎi	a sea of cloud
雲集	yúnjí	come together in crowds
雲氣	yúnqì	thin, floating cloud
雲雀	yúnquè	skylark
雲霧	yúnwù	cloud and mist
雲霄	yúnxiāo	the skies
雲霞	yúnxiá	rosy clouds

Each Character A Picture the Chinese Written Language

雲消霧散
yún xiāo wù sàn
The clouds melt and the mists disperse.
i.e., vanish in the air
過眼雲煙
guò yǎn yún yiān
as transient as a fleeting cloud
雲出無心
yún chū wú xīn
The cloud arises without design.
雲開見日
yún kāi jiàn rì
dispel the clouds and see the sun.

Example:

飛機在雲層的上面飛行。
Fēijī zài yúncéng de shàngmian fēixíng.
The plane is flying above the clouds.

一個漢字一幅畫

$$zhī$$
(know; be aware
of; knowledge)

知

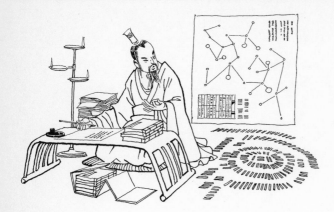

This character is a combination of (大) "arrow" and (ㅂ) "mouth", implying that what one knows well can be spoken very quickly (like an arrow).

知道	zhīdào	know
知己	zhījǐ	intimate friend
知覺	zhījué	consciousness; intuition
知名	zhīmíng	well-known; famous
知識	zhīshi	knowledge
知音	zhīyīn	a friend keenly appreciative of one's talents
知足	zhīzú	be content with one's lot

Each Character A Picture the Chinese Written Language

知己知彼
zhī jǐ zhī bǐ
know yourself as well as the enemy
i.e., know both sides

知恥近乎勇
zhī chǐ jìn hū yǒng
Feeling shame is close to bravery.

知法犯法
zhī fǎ fàn fǎ
deliberately flout the law
i.e., to know the law and violate it

知易行難
zhī yì xíng nán
To know is easy, to do is difficult.

知其不可為而為之
zhī qí bù kě wéi ér wéi zhī
to do something even while knowing it is impossible to succeed

知其然，不知其所以然
zhī qí rán, bù zhī qí suó yǐ rán
to know it is so, but not why it is so

知人者智，自知者明
zhī rén zhě zhì, zì zhī zhě míng
He who knows others is learned and he who knows himself is wise.

Example:

你要知道，如果你想成功，就得更努力。
Nǐ yào zhīdao, rúguǒ ní xiǎng chénggōng, jiù děi gèng nǔlì.
You'll have to try harder, you know, if you want to succeed.

一個漢字一幅畫

zhǐ

(stop)

止

From the oracle bones, we can see that (屮) characterizes the representation of a foot with the toes towards the left, and the heel to the right, so the original meaning of 止 is for "foot". But when the feet don't move then they "stop"; hence 止 has been extended to mean "stop" and this has replaced the original meaning of "foot".

止步	zhǐbù	halt; stop
止境	zhǐjìng	end; limit
止咳	zhíké	relieve a cough
止渴	zhíkě	quench one's thirst
止痛	zhǐtòng	relieve pain
止息	zhǐxī	cease; stop
止血	zhíxiě	stop bleeding

Each Character A Picture the Chinese Written Language

止步不前
zhǐ bù bù qián
stop the steps and no longer go ahead
i.e., standstill
止戈為武
zhǐ gē wéi wǔ
To stop the use of weapons and avoid war is truly military.
止水不波
zhí shuǐ bù bō
Still water does not have ripples.
i.e., a quiet mind
止謗莫若自修
zhǐ bàng mò ruò zì xiū
Nothing stop gossip as correcting one's own way.

Example:

我們的爭論到此為止吧。
Wǒmen de zhēnglùn dào cǐ wéi zhǐ ba.
Let's stop our argument here.

zhōng

(center; middle)

中

中 is also a pictograph character which shows a pole with some decorative streams (掌). In the middle there is a 口 indicating where the center is.

中餐	zhōngcān	Chinese food
中草藥	zhōngcǎoyào	Chinese herbal medicine
中等	zhōngděng	middling; medium
中國	Zhōngguó	China
中立	zhōnglì	neutrality
中秋節	zhōngqiūjié	the Chinese Mid-Autumn Festival
中心	zhōngxīn	center; core
中學	zhōngxué	middle school
中文	zhōngwén	Chinese language

中流砥柱
zhōng liú dǐ zhù
firm rock in midstream
i.e., a tower of strength

中外古今
zhōng wài gǔ jīn
both ancient and modern, Chinese and foreign

中飽私囊
zhōng bǎo sī náng
line one's pocket with public funds or other people's money

中西合璧
zhōng xī hé bì
a good combination (blending) of Chinese and Western elements

中庸之道
zhōng yōng zhī dào
the doctrine of the mean

中看不中用
zhōng kàn bù zhōng yòng
be pleasant with eyes, but not agreeable to the palate

Example:

園子的中間有一棵大樹。
Yuánzi de zhōngjiān yǒu yì kē dà shù
There is a big tree in the center of the garden.

(many; numerous)

Referring once again to ancient inscriptions found on the oracle bones, we find that 眾 was comprised of two parts: the upper part is "the sun" (⊖) and the lower part represents three people bending over working (彳彳), this being the original form and meaning of 眾. As it developed through time the sun above the three people turned into an eye shape (⌒), seeming to suggest a big eye watching over many people working. So "many" is the original meaning of 眾.

眾多	zhòngduō	multitudinous
眾人	zhòngrén	everybody
眾生	zhòngshēng	all living creatures
眾望	zhòngwàng	people's expectations

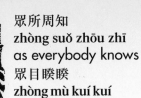

眾所周知
zhòng suǒ zhōu zhī
as everybody knows

眾目睽睽
zhòng mù kuí kuí
The eyes of the masses are fixed on somebody or something.

眾矢之的
zhòng shī zhī dí
target of public criticism

眾望所歸
zhòng wàng suǒ guī
to enjoy popular confidence

眾志成城
zhòng zhì chéng chéng
collective purpose forming a fortress

Example:

俗話説：眾人拾柴火焰高。
Sú huà shuō: zhòngrén shíchái huǒyàn gāo.
When all people add fuel the flames rise high.

zhōu
(administrative
division)

州

The ancient character of 州 was formed simply by adding a circle in the middle of 川, depicting land (or an island) in the center of a "river" (㣴) . The original meaning of this character was "land for living in the river". Later all the "three streams" of the "river" were added by the "land", and the three circles have turned into three dots. "關關雎鳩，在河之州", a verse from the poem "關雎" from the *Book of Songs* "詩經", written three thousand years ago, provides us a beautiful and imaginative way to learn this character.

九州	jiǔzhōu	a poetic name of China
神州	shénzhōu	the Division Land (also a poetic name of China)

只許州官放火，不許百姓點燈
zhí xǔ zhōu guān fàng huǒ,
bù xǔ bǎi xìng diān dēng
While the magistrates were allowed to
burn down the house, the common people
were forbidden even to light lamps.
i.e., The powerful can do what they want,
the weak are not allowed to do anything.

Example :

美國一共有五十一個州。
Měiguó yí gòng yǒu wǔshíyī ge zhōu.
There are altogether 51 administrative division in America.

zǐ 子

(son)

In the aracle bones the character depicts a child with three hairs growing on its head (㞢). Later it developed into another shape like new-born baby with legs swaddled in cloth bands and two arms waving (우), evoking a lively image of a baby.

子女	zínǚ	son and daughter
子弟	zǐdì	young generations
子孫	zǐsūn	descendants
子夜	zǐyè	midnight
獨生子	dúshēngzǐ	an only son
父子	fùzǐ	father and son

子肖其父
zǐ xiāo qí fù
The son is the very image of his father.

子子孫孫
zí zǐ sūn sūn
descendants

子孫後代
zǐ sūn hòu dài
generations to come

Example:

她的子女都在香港工作。
Tā de zí nǚ dōu zài Xiānggǎng gōngzuò.
Her sons and daughters are all working in Hong Kong.

一 個 漢 字 一 幅 畫

zì

(self)

自

自 is a pictograph of a nose (皏) which is seen from the front with nostrils and a bridge. So, originally it represented the nose. As Chinese people indicate "myself" by pointing to the nose, hence the meaning of this character became "self" or "oneself", and the original meaning for nose is no longer used.

自愛	zì'ài	self-respect
自白	zìbái	make clear of one's meaning or position
自卑	zìbēi	be self-effacing; insecure
自稱	zìchēng	to call onself; profess to be (sth.)
自從	zìcóng	since
自大	zìdà	self-important
自動	zìdòng	voluntarily; automatic
自費	zìfèi	at one's own expense
自負	zìfù	think highly of oneself
自己	zìjǐ	oneself
自覺	zìjué	conscious

自顧不暇
zì gù bù xiá
be unable even to fend for oneself
i.e., much less look after others

自告奮勇
zì gào fèn yǒng
offer to undertake (a difficult or dangerous task)
i.e., volunteer to do sth. difficult

自給自足
zì gěi zì zú
self sufficiency

自命不凡
zì mìng bù fán
consider oneself no ordinary being

自欺欺人
zì qī qī rén
deceive oneself as well as others

自強不息
zì qiáng bù xī
make unremitting efforts to improve oneself

自食其果
zì shí qí guǒ
eat one's own bitter fruit
i.e., reap what one has sown

自以為是
zì yǐ wéi shì
consider oneself (always) in the right

Example:

我是自費來讀書的。
Wǒ shì zìfèi lái dúshū de.
I came to study at my own expense.

$$zuǒ$$

(left) 左

左 is a drawing of a left hand. In the oracle bones, the shape of this character is same as the character "right hand" ( ), except the fingers are reaching in the opposite direction. Later a drawing of a carpenter's ruler ( ) was added under the hand, then it became a composite representation with a left hand holding a tool ( ). This indicates "to help" or "to help working", which was the original meaning of the character.

左邊	zuǒbiān	the left
左鋒	zuǒfēng	left forward
左面	zuǒmiàn	the left side
左派	zuǒpài	the left wing
左傾	zuǒqīng	left-leaning; inclined towards revolution
左手	zuóshǒu	the left hand
左右	zuǒyòu	the left and right sides; around
左證	zuǒzhèng	evidence

左顧右盼
zuǒ gù yòu pàn
glance right and left

左右逢源
zuǒ yòu féng yuán
be able to achieve success one way or another

左右為難
zuǒ yòu wéi nán
in a dilemma

左右開弓
zuǒ yòu kāi gōng
shoot first with one hand, then with the other
i.e., kick with both feet

左支右絀
zuǒ zhī yòu chù
not have enough money to cover the expenses
i.e., be unable to cope with a situation

Example:

去機場的車站就在金鐘廊的左邊兒。
Qù jīchǎng de chēzhàn jiù zài Jīnzhōng Láng de zuǒbiānr.
The bus stop to the airport is to the left of Queensway.

一 個 漢 字 一 幅 畫

Index

Each Character A Picture the Chinese Written Language